WOMEN & WORK

RESORT CARETAKER

Mary Anderson, 64, lives in a first aid station atop an 8,000-foot mountain. She has been caretaker of a mountain ski resort in the summer and on the ski patrol in the winter for the past 17 years.

I love the mountain. Since I have been here, I can't think of a place I would rather be. I love to do things to keep it beautiful and a pleasant place to be. The mountain has been good for me. The things I do can be called a labor of love. The hikers and skiers, young and old, summer and winter, reflect the spirit of well being and ecstasy. They tell me how they wish they could have a job like mine.

I feel comfortable with challenges, testing myself mentally and physically, finding new strengths and being able to tackle the almost impossible tasks without the aid of man or machine. Feeling no fear in being alone while Mother Nature does her thing . . . blinding blizzards, wind, rain, lightning, bugs. I live with the bare necessities up here on the mountain with running spring water, a gas refrigerator, and a generator for electricity, although I prefer a kerosene lamp for light. I like the feeling of getting along without civilization's comforts and living a simple life. The more things you have, the more there is to do and worry about. I've lived out of a backpack long enough to know how completely free you can feel from mundane, boring, daily living. One of my favorite quotes is Ellen Burstyn's: "What a loverly surprise to discover how unlonely alone can be."

Before coming to the mountain 17 years ago, I was married and worked in the Los Angeles garment district as a seamstress and designer's assistant making expensive designer clothes. I would ski every chance I could, and one night I said to my husband, "What I'd like to do is retire from my job and turn into a ski bum." I signed up for ski mountaineering training, became a professional ski patroller in 1973 and joined the staff at the Mount Waterman ski resort. I took a survival course after becoming a ski patroller and spent five weeks with the bare necessities in the wilderness, walking 350 miles. After that, I felt like I could lick my weight in wild cats, and that I was one leg into developing myself for the outdoor life.

Five years ago, my husband divorced me after 39 years of a good marriage and left me destitute. We lived an upper middle class existence with the nice home, swimming pool and all the things that everybody dreams of having. Since then, I have learned that I can accomplish things by myself and I have faith in myself. Now, I feel great being on the mountain. I have four grown children and 19 grandchildren living in California, Utah, and Virginia, so I'm on the telephone a lot. The one difficulty of my mountain home is that when my family wants to visit, there's no place for them to stay and I no longer have the swimming pool and the trampoline for the grandchildren that came with the nice big home.

In winter, I spend my days on the slopes keeping watch for injured skiers, providing emergency medical care if necessary. Just before dark each day, we do a sweep of the slopes to make sure all the skiers are accounted for and no one is lost. Sometimes I forget I'm an old lady because I don't have any aches and pains, not the way I used to before I got into skiing. I love the cold, the pure air and the drinking water, I think that's what keeps me healthy. In my spare time I like to stay creative. I sew and put quilt tops together with a treadle sewing machine that works like a charm.

The owner of the ski lift, Lynn Newcomb, has encouraged me and trusts me in my job. A man who can recognize a woman when she does something good and acknowledge it is a real man — and that separates the men from the boys. You never know what's going to happen from one day to the next up here, that's why I love my life. Sometimes, I think it's almost miraculous the way that I feel!

To: Kelly
From: Mark   11/89

WOMEN & WORK

PHOTOGRAPHS
- AND -
PERSONAL WRITINGS

Text Edited by Maureen R. Michelson

Photographs Edited by Michael R. Dressler & Maureen R. Michelson

NEWSAGE PRESS

Women & Work

Address inquiries to
NewSage Press
P.O. Box 41029
Pasadena, California
91104

Second Edition 1988

Printed in Japan

Library of Congress
Catalog Card Number:
86-62398

ISBN 939165-01-5

**Best Book for
Young Adults**

*–American Library
Association, 1987*

If it wasn't for the women, women
We would not be living, living
We would not be joyful, singing
Loving and beloved women

If it wasn't for the women
What would we do?
We wouldn't have
Health or strength or beauty
We wouldn't have a home
And we wouldn't have food
If it wasn't for the work
Of the women.

If it wasn't for the women
What would we do?
We wouldn't have
Art or craft or music
We wouldn't have love
And we wouldn't have truth
If it wasn't for the work
Of the women

— Alix Dobkin

ACKNOWLEDGEMENTS

Thinking of the women in my life who have contributed to this book in a thousand ways, weaving their lives into mine and into the life of this book. Most importantly, my Mother, Ruth Paczesny Michelson, who has spent a lifetime working with little fanfare; raising six children and loving them. She has always believed in me.

For my sister, Lorraine, whose growing love and support have been a source of comfort for me in our family. For the sisters Life has given me, my friends . . . they are all gifts. The friendship, encouragement, and dreams they offer inspire and strengthen me, daily. I am grateful to be in their presence.

For the long line of women in my family — the grandmothers, great grandmothers, the ancient ones who are no longer remembered — whose hearts and hands toiled many lifetimes, preparing the paths for today's women.

For my nieces, tomorrow's young women who will carry on. May they be inspired by the words and photographs in this book, and always believe in themselves and their dreams.

For the women in this book who so courageously trusted and shared parts of their lives for all to read. I am honored . . . inspired . . . proud.

Maureen R. Michelson

When I sat down to write this dedication, all sorts of important names with dust from the past, came forward and stared me in the face.

The dust is not because they have been forgotten . . . they just aren't within my daily contact any longer. I'm not trying to insult or hurt anyone . . . every treasure has dust on it, once in a while, because it *has* been around for so long.

Then there was the list of people who *are* in my life, almost daily, to consider. My life would not be complete without their care and understanding in very large dosages. These people are appreciated beyond the words in my heart and they know it! Then there are the treasures still to be discovered in future projects and in my own daily life.

All three groups have had their influences in me, so I'm taking this opportunity to thank these people for being there through all my stages of growth . . . so far. Lieux Dressler, Morris Repass, Timothy James, Julie Klingmann, Marty Haymaker, D. Gorton, Mr. "G", Leigh Garmon, Daniel Dressler, The Bungalow Heaven Crew, Mrs. Day (my third grade teacher), Gary Spoerle, Maureen Michelson and all the "Top Knots." And all the treasured people I've met since the printing of this book . . . thank you for your newness.

Michael Dressler

CONTENTS

INTRODUCTION

Women in the work force is a subject that has been analyzed and categorized by countless experts and academicians in numerous books. But rarely are women given the opportunity to speak for themselves, in their own words, about their work and what it means in the context of their lives. When they are listened to, they usually have to be qualified or recognized or somehow famous. For this book, we sought out women who were not famous although they may be accomplished or noted in their particular field. We wanted to avoid the limelight and seek out the "average" woman. However, we've since learned that each woman is far from average in the daily heroics of her life, even though she may never receive a moment's recognition in history.

It is difficult to represent the great variance of work that women do; it would take an encyclopedic effort to show the full spectrum of "women's work," which is essentially *all* work. Most of the women represented in this book were chosen randomly with no criteria for a certain political leaning or level of consciousness regarding women's issues. Traditional work as well as nontraditional work situations are included since they are all part of working women's lives in the United States.

Each woman was asked to write, as honestly as she could, about herself and her work and the issues that concern her. The door was open for each woman to share her reality, whatever that might be. There were common threads among most of the women; relationships, children, money, and for those in nontraditional work, dealing with male workers. There is also the unique history of each woman, the struggles and successes, that have brought her to this point in her life. What we learned is that stereotypes — of any kind — just don't hold when you take the time to listen to an individual. That behind all of those endless government statistics on women in the workplace are human beings, each with a history.

Experience sharing is powerful — quickly cutting through the distant, nonfeeling, objectifying of our world. With encouragement, most were able to go beyond the sur-face niceties and share the harder parts, whether creatively figuring out how to juggle children and work, or carrying on after a divorce or death in the family. They also shared the inspiration of persisting with their dreams. We are honored with the trust these women extended in sharing themselves openly with strangers — taking the risk of putting a part of themselves on paper for thousands to read.

Unquestionably, the 1980's is a time of great revolution in the work force, primarily because women are present in unprecedented numbers. Almost half of today's employed in the United States are women, in addition to the millions of unrecognized women working as homemakers. In the process of this book, we heard from many women sharing their stories and concerns. Many addressed these social issues, but in their own voices with their own experiences. They may not have been armed with the latest statistic that says "one-third of all families maintained by women have incomes below the poverty level," but they do say, "It's so difficult to make ends meet."

There are legitimate, unavoidable concerns for working women today that cannot be refuted, and require far-reaching social changes. Primary concerns among working women are pay equity and childcare. Whether college graduates or high school dropouts, women earn about 60 cents for every dollar their male counterparts are paid; a ratio that has existed since 1939. And more than half of all mothers in this country are working women, with more than eight-and-a-half million children under age six (a number greater than the population of New York City.) Childcare seems to be largely left up to parents with little support from government or the working world at large. As for homemakers who maintain a home on a 24-hour basis, they are struggling just to be recognized as legitimate workers, let alone get paid for their work.

Nearly half of today's employed in the U.S. are women and there are few working situations they have not at least pioneered. As women move into nontraditional jobs in greater numbers, there are a myriad of issues around working relationships between women and men. The concerns vary greatly, from one woman who says "the biggest objection I heard when I was hired was that the men would have to shut the bathroom door," to another who was told flat out she wouldn't be hired "because you're a woman." Throughout this book many of these issues are talked about, but with the power of the individual experience.

We had the idea for a book on women and their work, but it was the energy from many people that gave this book its life. We hold a special appreciation for all those who contributed, whether or not their work is represented. The interest, enthusiasm, and belief of hundreds of people in this project, *Women & Work, Photographs and Personal Writings,* is now what you hold in your hands.

Walt Mancini

POLITICIAN

"Able" Mable Thomas, 28, is State Representative for the 31st District in Atlanta, Georgia.

I ran for office in a low to moderate income area in Atlanta, and the power structure said that it would be impossible for me to get elected in this district as a grassroots candidate. First, they said, you don't have any money, and secondly, you cannot defeat a 19 year incumbent. Nevertheless, I was able to mobilize my community by pulling together young people, retired persons, senior citizens, unemployed persons, homeowners, public housing tenants, college students, businesses, and churches to successfully launch a grassroots movement to get me elected to this seat. There were four persons in the primary, and I emerged as the front runner to face the incumbent, Mrs. Grace Towns Hamilton, who was also the first Black woman elected to the Georgia General Assembly. The community elected me state representative by 71% of the vote.

It was about timing, everything is about timing. It was time for people to be open to a new leadership. You only have to be 18 years of age in order to work as a state representative, so, it wasn't like being elected couldn't have been done by another person. There's a mystique about politics that you have to be older, settled in your job, and know everybody. Basically, when Jesse Jackson ran for president, he dispelled those myths. He made people more open to accept the fact that I was a young person running, so I was elected at age 26, and the youngest state representative in Georgia. At the time I was elected, I was also into my second term as vice president of the student government at Georgia State University, and doing graduate work in public administration. I resigned my school office to devote more time to being a state representative, and at the time, I was also Jesse Jackson's top delegate from Georgia to the Democratic National Convention.

Some of the obstacles you go through as a woman or Black are more subtle than overt. I can't just name a specific incident, but rather look at the whole institution of Georgia. We are basically a conservative state, and people who are in the Georgia Legislature are basically white, rural, males. A lot of them have been property owners and their families were involved in politics. So, they've been in power for a long time. Even though you might not be able to see racism overtly, it clearly exists in the Georgia Legislature. It goes through a seniority system and Black people are just moving into it. Seniority makes it hard to move through the system because you can't move faster than the seniority. Presently, there are 21 Black representatives out of 180 and six of those are women. And in the Georgia Senate, there are only six Black men out of 56.

The old boys network is there and I'm not part of it, and I'm not part of the back-room decisions, but it still comes down to one thing — they still have to deal with me because I have a vote. They will have to come to me and ask my support on something, but I'm not part of that real decision making. I deal with it as if everything is cool, but then I also take a principled position and don't sell out regardless of whether or not my opinion is a popular one. In the whole system there are a lot of illusions of inclusion. But I'd rather know where I am at, and then they have to deal with me because my principled position is in their face rather than for them to think I'm part of the good ol' boy system.

Presently, I serve on the House Education, Special Judiciary and Industrial Relations Committees. My committee assignments relate directly to my interests and community involvement, and the need assessments of my district, which I am very pleased with. As the youngest state representative, who was elected by the people without the power structure's blessings, I expected some resistance from the old guard leadership in the Georgia General Assembly. However, I had a very successful first term due to the fact that I refused to accept their negativity, and consistently worked to project a positive image. I spent my first year listening and building networks with fellow legislators, and was able in the second year of my first term to author and pass three major pieces of legislation that related to housing development and health care. I also co-sponsored several pieces of legislation relating to urban enterprise zones, fair taxation, and minority work programs.

I feel very strongly about my faith in God, commitment to the people, and determination to improve the quality of life of Georgia's citizenry. I love and accept my responsibility for leadership. I know that the youth are the key to the future so I actively support youth development, quality housing and education, and economic development. I am unopposed this year for re-election and will be entering my second term.

Cheryl Bray

REHABILITATION NURSE

Susie Matz, 40, is a nurse working for the past ten years in a hospital, primarily in rehabilitation.

I was to marry and graduate from nursing school in 1968 when Life's biggest roadblock fell upon me, an airplane crash. Immediately waking up in the airplane, I knew I was a paraplegic. I couldn't feel anything from the waist down. There was no conceivable way I knew how I was going to live this way. At 22 years of age, I was already angry, misread from my childhood, and the middle of two brothers that I couldn't compete with. Now I was faced with no control over bowel and bladder functioning, no more orgasms, atrophying muscles, physical inability. It was too much to cope with. The only way out was to kill myself!

Sadness and depression set in, I couldn't face a soul — I would not go out of the house. How was an ordinary person with a low self-esteem going to battle and come ahead of something like this? Now came the challenge; to sink or swim. Piloted by the anger, I went on to make what I thought to be life's most difficult adjustment. One day, after viewing the movie, "The Other Side of the Mountain," I decided I had more left to use after this accident.

Slowly, I learned how to control my body and get around in a wheelchair. I went back to school, finished my education as a Registered Nurse (R.N.) and tried passing the boards. I failed. Years later I tried the L.V.N. (Licensed Vocational Nurse) boards and passed. No one would hire me as an L.V.N. so I sat on the bed with all the textbooks from school and read and read. Six hours a day for six months. I retook the R.N. test and *passed!*

Getting a job was the next hurdle. They all said,"You can't do the physical things required by a nurse from a wheelchair." Finally, a CETA program (Comprehensive Employment Training Act) opened at a hospital near my home. After two years of fruitless hunting, a job! "Come to work on Monday," they said on the phone. "You're going to be a patient representative." I knew what it was like to be a patient, now I had to learn the hospital administrative side of things to balance my perspective.

Two years later, the discharge coordinator job in the rehab center opened, and I was going to where I belonged . . . helping people with disabilities get a start on their new way of life. It's hard working on rehab. My job is to insure when a patient is discharged, that they and their families have been educated about their disability. I have always felt I shouldn't be real vocal because I don't represent all handicapped people. On the other hand, I have found health care professionals have poor insight into the care and lifestyle of a person with my problem. Reality orientation is difficult and often the staff would try to ignore me by treating me like a patient. They can't ignore me, you see, I'm one of them. Hopefully, the patients can see me come to work and realize there is life after disability.

My father died at age 61. Shortly after his death, I was hospitalized for seven months with an infection in my leg. Through it all, through life's many losses, I stayed alive and "kept my meat on the treadmill of life." I came to find strengths in myself I never knew I had. My hope is to touch souls with others; to focus on the strengths, abilities, and love in myself and in others. When I come down the halls of the hospital, singing a familiar song, and an aphasic stroke patient (who has lost the use of language) finishes the last line of the song, you know you touched souls. For that minute, you hope the patient forgot they were in a hospital and knew they could return to the life they knew. To help them focus on the fact that the doctor doesn't do it all, that they have the control over their own destiny.

It feels like an honor and a privilege to open the door each morning and see the sunshine on the flowers, to be able to get my chair in the car and drive to work. The patients at work are facing what I faced 18 years ago. To put a song in their hearts and hope in their souls, that's the goal. My career has helped me to grow personally and professionally. My self-esteem is walking again! No one could tell me I had any exceptional qualities, the wheelchair proved me wrong. I had to come to the test or sit in my room and wither. God knows I don't forget swinging my legs over the side of the bed and walking to the bathroom and peeing — but God also knows life's other rewards he has brought to me.

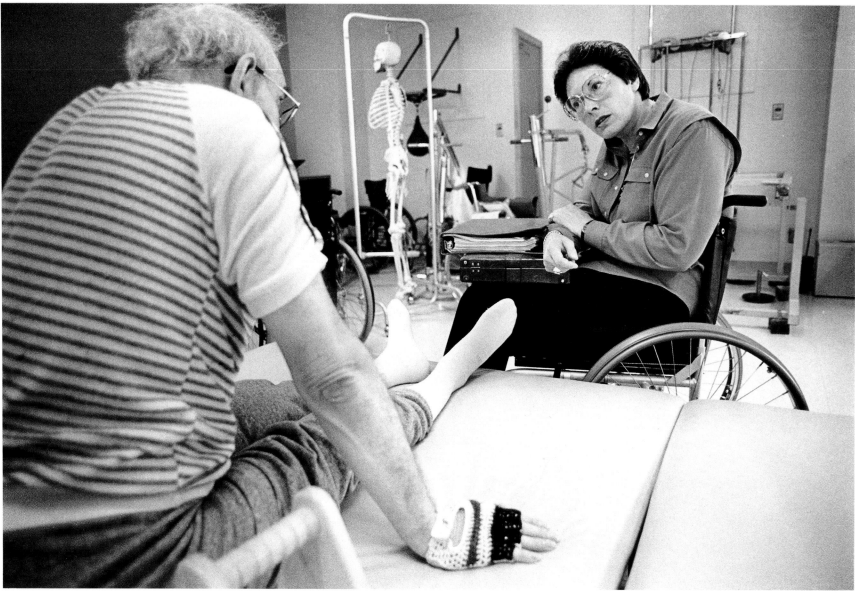

Jeff Share

AUTO DISMANTLER

Jennifer Anne Johnson, 24, works in an auto wrecking yard.

Working in a wrecking yard is a man's job for sure, but I believe that if you have the knowledge of the tools of the trade, it makes up for the loss of physical strength. In my job I am usually covered in grease, but men still ask me, "What's a pretty girl like you doing in a place like this?" I just say, "I'm trying to make a living."

The men I work with are behind me 100 percent. They think it's great and say they can relate to me more than most women they date because I really know what it is to grab a beer and say, "I'm tired cuz I worked my butt off."

I really enjoy my work and think that women would accomplish more if they would worry less about what some men or commercials say . . . and worry more about just being proud to be a woman, no matter what you do cuz I think I look just fine with or without the grease.

Hugh Steimle

ORCHESTRA CONDUCTOR

JoAnn Falletta, 32, is a conductor with the Denver Chamber Orchestra, the Queens Philharmonic in New York, and Associate Conductor with the Milwaukee Symphony. She also works with the Bay Area Women's Philharmonic.

My music studies began when I was seven years old, and I played guitar, piano and cello. About the time I was 12, my parents started taking me to concerts and I fell in love with the orchestra. I never had experienced anything like that, to see a group of people working together to create something so special. It was then that I decided I wanted to be able to shape what a group like that was doing.

When I first went to the Conservatory at the age of 18, it was a whole year before they would let me major in conducting because they said no woman had ever had a success in the field. They didn't want to encourage me to be a conductor because they didn't hold out any chance of my ever doing that. It took me a year to convince them. That was difficult because that was the first resistance I had ever encountered and it surprised me. I just kept doing as well as I could in my courses and telling them yes, I was interested and I recognize that it's never been done. I was also lucky that a new teacher came to the school who was perhaps a little younger and more understanding about the possibilities.

Today, there is probably some reservation on the part of the major level symphonies, particularly the older people in those symphonies and the older board members, to a young American woman conducting. I still think that needs to be broken down and the way to do that is through professionalism and hard work. What's more troubling to me, more than being a woman, is being an American. On the highest levels of music making in the United States we are very prejudiced against our own home-grown products, and there's always a preference given to European conductors because they come from a different cultural background than our own. I think it's an American inferiority complex that we've always emulated Europe and I find that frustrating.

Working on the major level, there are only two conductors who are women, myself and Katherine Comet, who is working with the Baltimore Symphony as an Associate Conductor. The two of us probably have what is considered the highest conduction positions held by women in this country. I am sure there are other women in conservatories who will be coming into the field, but so far it's been very limited. For the last couple of years I have been extremely busy because I have three orchestras and I am conducting about 170 concerts a year, which is unbelieveable when I thought of what I would be doing ten years ago. There were times when I was just starting out that I was very depressed and I knew my parents always wanted me to go to law school. As little as five years ago they'd say, "Why not think about law school?" Conducting is such an iffy career; I never knew if it was going to work for me. But I always felt that somehow I would make it because I knew I wanted it so much.

I feel that it is a tremendous privilege to be working as a musician in the United States. There is potential, a desire, an openness to new ideas that is a challenge and a stimulant to me. Of course, there are disappointments and difficulties, but the moments of magic more than make up for them. To hear a Mozart symphony take shape in your hands, to see an orchestra work with all its heart and talent towards the creation of something beautiful; to feel that together we have moved and uplifted our audience beyond the cares and troubles of their everyday lives — all this makes working as a conductor the realization of my most cherished dream. One doesn't choose music, music chooses you — and fills your life with pain, frustration, loneliness, insecurity, passion, turmoil, happiness, grief, anxiety, intensity, peace, satisfaction, dissatisfaction, longing, desire, hard work, and the most incredible joy I could ever imagine.

Nita Winter

COAL MINER

Donna Jean Ventresco, 42, has been a coal miner for a company in Pennsylvania for the past seven years.

I grew up with coal mine talkers. My father started when he was 14 and was a miner for 46 years. And my uncles worked there and I guess you could say their talking about it made me go for the job when I got older. I worked two weeks before my mother found out. She wasn't too happy with the fact that I was in the mines. She said that was no place for women. My husband Chuck, who's a truck driver, was worried about me for a long time, but once I told him that I'm not scared to enter the mines, he stuck right by me.

I had been out of a job for six months when I got the job at the mines. Before that, I made minimum wage at a drapery factory. I bugged a superintendent at the coal company for a year before I got the job, but I was going to get in them mines. He kicked me out of his office a few times. He probably said, "Hire her, and hire her at another mine because I don't want to see her." Two of my friends said, "Women don't belong in the mines. You'll never make it, Jean." So I said, "Yes I will. I'll bet you anything. If it kills me, I'll make it."

Well, I'll tell you about the mines. At first, I was scared that I wouldn't be able to do the work. But once I really got to understand and operate the machines, it made it a lot easier. I don't hate my job at all. I get along with everyone at the mines and we help each other as much as we can. The money, about $14 an hour, and benefits are too good to let go of and that helps you keep going. My work includes running the "scoop," a machine that hauls supplies and picks up loose coal; operating a shuttle car for transporting coal; helping to install 18-foot wooden beams to support the roof; and helping the bolter. The hard part at the end of the shift is climbing 200 steps to get out of the mines . . . you're real tired at the end of the day.

When I first started working in the mines, you name it, the men said it. They said, "You're a woman, we're gonna have to do the work for you." But after I started working with them, there's no problem, once you've proved yourself. Now, the crew and I all joke around and that really helps a lot. It makes the shift go faster and the work a lot easier. It's like we all stick together. My worst experience in the mines was when a rock had fallen on a crew member and the men lifted the rock and I pulled him out from underneath it. He died two days later. It had me shocked up for awhile.

My dreams I've had since I was 16 years old were to have a good husband, children, own my house, and have a Corvette. Well, since then I got all of those things and I'm very happy with my life. I'm a mother of five children from the ages of 18 years through 24 years, and a grandmother of four. I got custody of my first grandson who is seven years old and I've had him since he was three. It was like starting over after I raised all five of mine, but he's worth it. I don't know if I'll retire after working 10 or 20 years in the mines. My family wants me to retire when 10 years are up, but I don't really know that yet.

FIREFIGHTER

Rosa Torres, 27, is one of nine women firefighters in Los Angeles.

"Oh, you work for the Fire Department? You must be a paramedic . . . no? Then you do administrative work, don't you?"

It's quite entertaining to see just how incredulous some people are at the thought of female firefighters. But on the other end of the scale are those (few) who become proud at what I have accomplished. I've been working as a firefighter for over two years now and I wouldn't trade it for the world.

My being a firefighter has not been easy, nor do I ever expect it to be. I am continuously proving myself and those I've not yet worked alongside are hard pressed to give affirmation to my credibility. Yet, I cannot think of anything more rewarding or fulfilling. I've filled a wide variety of positions. Everything from private secretary to telephone installer to dancer, and *nothing* compares with being a firefighter.

It's a lot tougher emotionally than any other type of job, but the guys here empathize. We all know what it's like to have to go into a burning building and step over dead bodies in hopes of reaching someone that may be alive. No one else can understand that. You come to know your co-workers very well, and your lives depend on each other. While everyone else is running out of a burning building, I am running in! My adrenalin starts pumping, my heart rate increases and my body knows it's time to go to work. This job demands that your body perform well beyond the limits your mind has put on it, and it does. The well being of lives and the preservation of property are at stake and it's up to me and my co-workers to protect them.

After a job well done, it's pats on the back, handshakes, and joviality all around. But when lives are lost the gloom hangs in the air and those most deeply affected can always find a sympathetic ear with compassionate understanding to help them through it. Our lives depend on each other which builds a very strong bond. On my shift there are 14 members — I'm the only female and they know they can depend on me to do my job and back them up. I feel I've gained 13 brothers.

Deborah Roundtree

MOTHER, WIFE, EDUCATOR

Patricia Lawhon, 62, photographed with seven of her ten daughters, and one granddaughter. She is the mother of 13 children.

I am the hardest-working woman I know, always have been. A fact unglamorous and immutable. As my 22-year-old daughter put it, "You're so chore-oriented." I like to think I haven't time enough to finish all the projects I've planned for this life; I can't be goofing off. The truth, of course, must lie between these views.

Over 40 years ago, when I graduated from college, I had vague career goals. It was war time, and within a year I was married, had a husband overseas, and was pregnant with the first of 13 children. I wallowed in the baby boom. (But not in that throw-uppy "meet your husband at the door in just a see-through cocktail apron" foolishness.) What fed the fervor of domesticity? Being Catholic and being an army wife. And I never questioned the admirableness of either state.

Good friends shared my views. We wanted the most attractive homes, the most achieving children, the most contented husbands, delicious meals, delightful parties. We were neighbors on army posts in North Carolina, Virginia, Maryland, Germany; and we must have seen ourselves as pioneer women crossing the plains together. We worked our tails off, but never for money. That would have been unthinkable. Our husbands were officers, our children were young, we pulled up stakes on very short notices. Our careers were being army wives. I worked harder than most because I had more to do — bigger quarters (more children). Bridge parties, cocktail parties, dinners — I didn't want to miss any. Of course, they demanded that I return the invitations. I've often thought I'm lucky that the things I most like to do involve staying home. (I'm very ungraceful; had I gone out for Ladies Golf, I'd have been a dud. *Ladies* golf. That says it; it was a world that smart women today just don't know.)

What didn't we do! Turn out beautiful clothes; I learned to cover shoes with fabric at Norfolk; refinish antiques (I refinished the wood on a station wagon built during the Korean War); make fruit cakes by the washtub-full, plant flowers, make rootbeer, run PTA meetings and scout troops. We weren't pollyannas, but we thought what we did was important, and we did it well. Sure, some wives slept around, started drinking before lunch, maybe even took drugs —not the ones I spent time with.

I do work for money now. I teach at a Jesuit university, and I love it. Sometimes I'm even asked to speak before a group that pays me. I went back for a Master's in English (to counter the disorientation of quitting cigarettes) and, by sheer chance, ended up teaching at a local junior college. Don't think this is any big success story. At the university I am part-time, that means I am not included in department meetings, I march last at commencements, etc. No ability, no enthusiasm, no popularity with students can change the status of a non-Ph.D. "lecturer." At my age, who would bother with a Ph.D.? I'd rather devote the time to writing. I don't wish to cavil; I do want women to know you never get it all. If you put off a career until you raise a family, accept the fact that you are unlikely to catch up.

Almost all my children have graduated from college now. One daughter is a lawyer, another a national park ranger. What I find surprising is that six are nurses, especially because I want to bolt when I see blood. My daughters claim I expected them to marry brain surgeons; I'm dead positive I never encouraged marriage at all. I do want them to have work they love. Women who spend their lives at work they hate are slaves. I tried to make housework creative — sheer numbers made a challenge out of motherhood. I admit that I'll like my life better when I'm freed from so much responsibility of homemaking. I love work, and I have a lot still to do. My book is two-thirds finished and I have three new courses slated for next year. I just pray I have enough years to finish some of the projects I have in mind.

Raisa Fastman

PILOT

Janis L. Keown Blackburn, 38, is a Second Officer with Eastern Airlines, and has been flying for nearly 20 years. Today, she is one of 30 women pilots (and 4500 male pilots) working for Eastern.

I think the beauty of flying is one of the most exciting parts of my work. To sit in the cockpit with those large windows, I get a great view. One of the most spectacular sights is taking off on a day with low clouds, fog, rain, the whole miserable thing. We climb through layer after layer of cold, gray clouds, and then all of a sudden at 18 or 20 thousand feet, we pop out of the top of the cloud layer to a bright blue sky and shining sun with billowy white clouds below. The sun is never so bright nor the sky so blue as when you come out the top like that.

Right after high school I began taking flying lessons while holding a fulltime job at a bank. I knew when I was little, maybe six years old, that I wanted to fly. I always liked airplanes, and would stop whatever I was doing when I heard one, and watch it go over . . . I still do. I think it's aviation in general. Either you love it or you hate it . . . very few people just like it a little bit. It was funny when I worked at the bank. Every Friday when we got paid, all the girls would go shopping and always had new clothes . . . and I had more hours in my log book. At Christmas or birthday time, people would ask what I wanted for a present and I'd always say, "An hour of flying." But other than presents, every cent came out of my own pocket for flying lessons.

I had been sending resumes and applications to Eastern Airlines for eight years before I got the job. Before that, I was a flight instructor for awhile, I flew for a commuter airline in New Jersey, also flying night freight, and then flying a 727 with a charter airline out of Minneapolis. But of course, none of them were major airlines, which is what I wanted. I told the interviewer at Eastern the only way you're going to stop reading my resumes is to hire me because I intended to just continue if they hadn't taken me then. It was a long road, and I had probably applied to all the airlines, but Eastern was the one I really wanted. So much of it with the airlines is luck, I guess. It depends whether they're hiring. I was just willing to wait that long because this is what I wanted to do.

Most of the airlines also have height requirements for their pilots and that was a hinderance because I'm a little bit shorter than the minimum 5'4". They made me fly the simulator with an engine failure right at take off, just as you're breaking ground. They wanted to make sure I could keep the plane going straight. I was able to do it, so they decided to hire me. I guess they figure you need so much leg to be able to reach the rudder peddles to keep an airplane going straight.

The reactions of the passengers is sometimes fun. Occasionally, little old ladies will say, "Oh, you're one of the pilots. I feel so much better knowing a lady is up there." People turn and look when I walk past. Many times, while deplaning, guys who look like they're in their early 20's say, "You're a pilot, hey, right on baby!" While we're flying, if I go in the cabin to fix something, many eyebrows raise. It's fun watching people watch me, and to see their reactions to me doing my job.

The job isn't the glamorous career many people might think. I have done a preflight during a hurricane with a downpour and 40 mph winds. I never dried 'til after we got to Palm Beach. The preflight must be done in rain, shine, snowstorm or cold and bitter night, and it's the second officer's job to do it. During the preflight, it's my time alone with the airplane. Eastern Airlines can make the payments, but when I'm the only one around, it's all mine. I talk to it and pat it and just enjoy my few minutes alone with such a marvelous thing of beauty.

Ilene Perlman

HOUSEKEEPER

Katie Sims, 71, is a housekeeper but she says she's "nobody's maid."

When I was a little girl in Mississippi, my mother used to cook a lot. I would follow her into the kitchen and keep it clean while she got it dirty cooking. Everytime I saw my mother doing something, I would help. That's how I got my start. At 19, I started to work on my own. I asked people if they knew anyone who needed a housecleaner. Then I started to work three jobs a day, and one at night in the bank cleaning the office 'til 11 p.m.

When I was 20, I got married to a man in the service. He sent for me, and I moved to California. I didn't work much while married, but that was not for too long. My husband died. Then I began to work a lot and I have since then.

I like to work, but I don't like it when I go into a house and the stove is all dirty and greasy. Sometimes people don't flush their toilets. It's hard to clean. It makes me tired. But, I have a lot of fun on the job. For instance, if a house I'm working in is dirty, I start singing a song. I don't get mad, and before I know it, the house is all clean. People love the way I clean. It makes me happy. I look forward to going to my job 'cause I feel like I'm going home.

I've been working for the same people for over 25 years. I'm dependable. People trust me. They give me nice things and they feed me well. I feed them well, too. I make an honest living, and I've always had enough to eat. I work seven days a week. I don't want any days off. Only Christmas day. People want to know why I am so happy on my job. I tell them it's because I love to work. But the thing I find the most disappointing about my job is when I ask for a raise and I don't get it. I feel that I work hard enough to get a raise.

Abigayle Tarsches

PIPING DESIGNER

Yoshie A. Cooper, 48, is a Piping Designer, building models of complex structures prior to their construction.

Born and raised in Japan, my technical career started in Tokyo as a tracer. Under the Japanese labor system, both male and female employees start at the bottom level and you work your way to the top. One must go through all the aspects of training. No short cuts, regardless of superior abilities. Thoroughness and neatness are most important in Japanese business. This system doesn't permit fakers and freeloaders. I was somewhat of a maverick because I soon left the Japanese employer to work for an American architectural firm that was doing designs for the United States Defense Department. I did architectural drafting under American and Japanese supervisors. There was no resentment against women in the U.S. firms; there were opportunities and rewards according to your ability.

In the spring of 1964, I married my American architectural supervisor, and in the fall of that year, migrated to the U.S. I spent two years studying English at college, adjusting to the culture, keeping home and raising flowers and building structures for the garden. I loved the "do-it-yourself" lumberyard and the "do-it-yourself" tools which gave me the courage to build two houses during the 1970's, from excavation to wallpapering.

After two years in the U.S., my former office asked me to work as an architectural draftsperson. This was my first encounter of freeloaders and fakers. There wasn't the old pride of workmanship that I had experienced in Japan. I soon discovered supervisors played favorite to some employees. They were usually the employees who had a "gift of gab." Being the boss' favorite in the U.S. doesn't mean you're the best qualified. In Japan, if you are a favorite, the entire company will support an exceptional employee.

In 1974, after 15 years of architectural drafting, I saw a newspaper ad for a piping designer. I applied for the position to be trained and was accepted. The work in piping was more gratifying than architectural drafting. The treatment to me was the same as for men, even though the ratio of female pipers is one to every 60 men. I personally don't experience any discrimination, I do the same job as the men. Projects are usually large and are needed, post haste. Consequently, there is a lot of rapid hiring and rapid layoff. This is not good for personal morale. It would be much better if we could diversify our experience, then we could work more efficiently with less people and wouldn't have the big layoffs. A family attitude is better than the job factory attitude.

Piping design model making has proven to be very helpful for the industry. Many of the petrochemical, sulfur and nuclear plants are so large and complex, the color-coded model designs are more effective in eliminating interferences and are easy to visualize and understand. There are fewer glitches in the design when you build a scale model. I always enjoy working with my hands and I have the patience for tedious details. When people ask me what my occupation is, I say, "Piping Designer." Ten out of ten people reply with a questionable "What?" Then I have to spell "p-i-p-e," piping designer . . .

Candace C. Allen

SPORTS JOURNALIST

Elizabeth Shanov, 33, is a Sports Journalist, covering Los Angeles-area sports for ABC Radio Network. Coverage of major events include the 1984 Summer Olympics, the Super Bowl, NBA Championships, home games for all the city's major sports teams, and more. She began her broadcasting career in 1975.

Assignment: Cover the NBA basketball game between the Los Angeles Lakers and the Utah Jazz at the Forum, Inglewood, CA.

6:30 p.m.: Arrive at Forum. Call the night producer in New York. "OK, I got it. You want interviews with two people from the winning team, one from the losing team. Let's hope for a fast game." Deadline: 10 p.m. Pacific time. The show goes on the air at 10:09 p.m.

7:38: Game starts.

7:50: This is going to be a blowout. The Lakers already have a huge lead.

8:05: Uh-oh, trouble. A Utah player is hurt. Game delayed. This deadline is definitely in jeopardy.

9:15: Lakers lead by 30 points. Pray for no fouls . . . fouls stop the clock and drag out the game.

9:38: Game ends. The coaches can keep the locker room closed to reporters for no more than ten minutes (NBA rules). Meeting the deadline is still possible.

9:40: Interview Jazz coach Frank Layden. A real stand-up comedian. He uses several obscenities in answering the question. It'll make a good tape for the "never-used-for broadcast blooper reel," but right now Liz needs clean language, and a pithy quote for the show. She gets it.

9:48: Rush into Laker locker room. Talk to head coach Pat Riley who comes up with a good quote quickly. More interviews with players.

9:58: A mad dash to the pressroom telephone. Tape rewinding as she runs. Liz remembers the exact answers from each of the players that she will send to the producer in New York. As she rewinds the tape, she notes the positions of those answers.

9:59: Connect the tape recorder to the phone with alligator clips. Connect the microphone into the tape recorder.

10:00: Call the producer. Relay names of the interviewees, how many points they scored, any pertinent facts about the quotes, and transmit the tape. Liz makes the deadline.

"Wow! You mean you get to go into the *locker rooms*?" That's always the first thing they want to know when they find out I'm a sports reporter. Well, yes, almost all professional sports teams in the United States have finally agreed that a female sports reporter deserves the same access to the players and coaches that a male reporter has. So, yes, I do get to go into most locker rooms. But people who think that a post-game interview in a sweaty, smelly, crowded clubhouse is a glamorous or titillating experience . . . well, they've never been there.

Actually, most players will either stay in their uniforms or wear towels during an interview. Sure, there are a few who try to embarass or shock women reporters by strutting around stark naked. I've found the best way to handle sophomoric behavior is to ignore it. That's not hard to do when you've got 20 minutes after the game to rush to the locker rooms, formulate your questions, persuade the game's pivitol players to say something cogent, then rush back to the pressroom to file your story. You simply don't have time for anything but your job.

I'm glad to be working in Los Angeles. For one thing, the sports teams here are winners. For another, women sports reporters aren't an oddity here. There are female sportswriters, television camera operators, photographers, and broadcasters. We've all been hit by flying athletic supporters (underwear, not fans) and called every sexist term for "woman" that's ever appeared in "Playboy." But when I was doused by champagne in a victory celebration . . . well, that's when I knew the players had decided, "She's ok. She belongs."

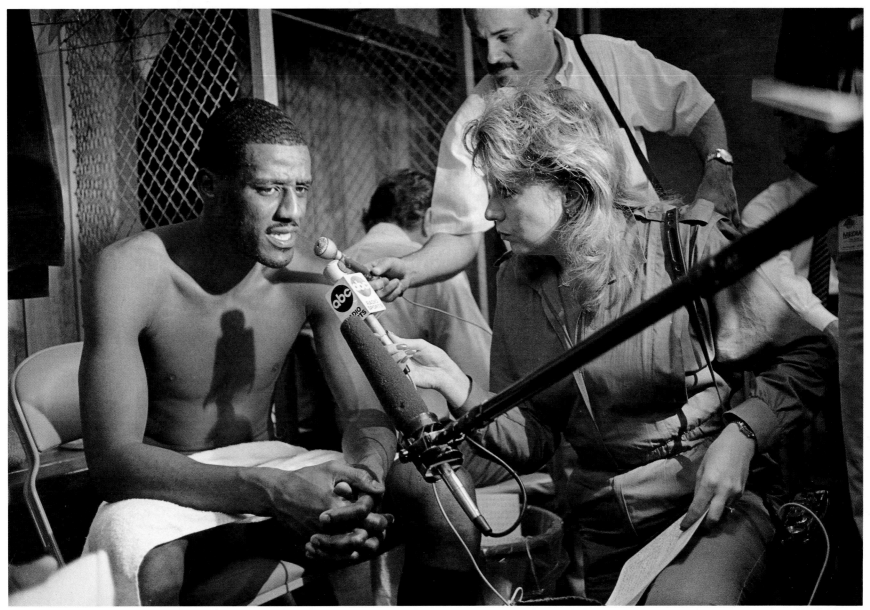

Walt Mancini

CITRUS PACKER

Lupe V. Reyes, 54, began packing oranges when she was 16 years old.

To write about myself, that is hard for me to do. I don't have much education because I had to quit school when I was young. I had lots of brothers and sisters to care for because my parents were not well. Being second to the oldest, I had to help out. At 16, I started working in a packing house packing oranges, and have worked in packing houses a long time. Oh, I have gotten other jobs, but it was not the same. So, I would quit and go back to the packing house. It is a good job, we work hard, but it is good.

When I first worked in oranges, it was for Blue Goose Packing House. I think we got 10¢ a box, but then the work was much harder. The way we packed the oranges was different and we used big wooden boxes that had a wooden divider in the middle. We didn't set these boxes on the line like we do today, but on small benches we had at our station. In the box we put 113 oranges on one side and 113 oranges on the other side. But the hard part was to wrap each orange in tissue paper and the little goose on the paper had to go right in the center so it would look good.

We could pack about 100 boxes a day, so maybe I would make $12 for the day. Now we use cardboard boxes and best of all, we don't wrap the oranges any more. The boxes are smaller so we can work much faster and make more money. We get about the same amount of money we did when I started in the packing houses, but now we can pack more. We get 12½¢ a box, and our minimum is 220 boxes a day. Lots of times, if you are strong, you can pack 220 boxes in the morning, and if you are still strong or young, you can do the same thing in the afternoon. If you don't make your minimum, the packing house pays minimum wage — they have to by law.

Oranges come in different sizes and we pack them that way, such as the small orange is a "no. 210" because 210 oranges fit into the box. The largest orange is a "no. 48" because 48 large oranges go into one box. In the packing house there are different lines with different size oranges on each line. We work each line 15 minutes, packing different sizes because we are paid by the box, and if we only pack small oranges, we would not make any money. So we change so that everyone gets a chance to pack the different sizes and make more money. The packed orange box weighs between 46 to 50 pounds each, and we each pack between 300 and 400 boxes a day. If we could pack 48's all day, I would be rich.

Now that I am older, I'm glad I don't have to lift the boxes very far. And I don't want to work 12 hours anymore. Being an orange packer is fun and it has its advantages because it is seasonal. I can be home with my kids in the summer, I am the mother of four and the grandmother of 14, so they don't have to stay with someone else. I really like my job and most of the other employees, and our boss is good to us.

Sharon Shoemaker

JUDGE

LaDoris Hazzard Cordell, 36, became the first Black woman judge in northern California in 1982.

There is a certain arrogance inherent to the notion that anyone should have the right to make decisions about the lives of other human beings. As I drove to court on the very first day of my judicial assignment, I kept thinking, "Who said that I could do this job anyway?" Now, I feel at home in the judiciary. The tasks involved challenge all of my faculties. It allows me to be creative. What I do and how I do it can dramatically alter the course of a person's life. And, I think, the fact that I am Black and female gives me even greater impact in my role as a judge. So often defendants appear before me presenting themselves as victims of society. Sometimes, indeed, they are. Often they are not. They all expect to be met by an older white male on the bench, and when they see me sitting there, it is as if the entire system has opened up before them. If I can be a judge, then maybe they can make a go of it. I become the incarnation of hope.

When I was working in Mississippi in 1967, I met my first Black woman lawyer. To this day, I do not know her name, but she impressed me tremendously with her courage and commitment. I think that being inspired by her, and by my parents who have been my perpetual source of inspiration, I decided to embark on a legal career. When I was admitted to Stanford Law School in 1971, I was one of two Black women in the school. There I was at one of the most prestigious universities in the country with my huge Afro, wondering if this was where I should be. I found many professors to be supportive and understanding. Indeed, some remain my mentors and good friends to this day.

My decision to enter the judiciary was the result of my search for new challenges. I had practiced law for six years, establishing myself as the first and only lawyer in my community. During that six year period, I returned to my alma mater Stanford to work as the Assistant Dean, and in 1982 I became a judge. I wish that my grandparents could see me now. They were incredibly proud people, filled with dignity and high aspirations. But I do not think that in their wildest dreams they imagined that their granddaughter would one day be a judge. When I get discouraged about the magnitude of social injustice or mourn the petty pace of societal change, I think about them.

I want to make a difference. I have had some wonderful life experiences. They have permitted me to do the things that I deem important; to have an impact, no matter how small, on the people with whom I share this planet.

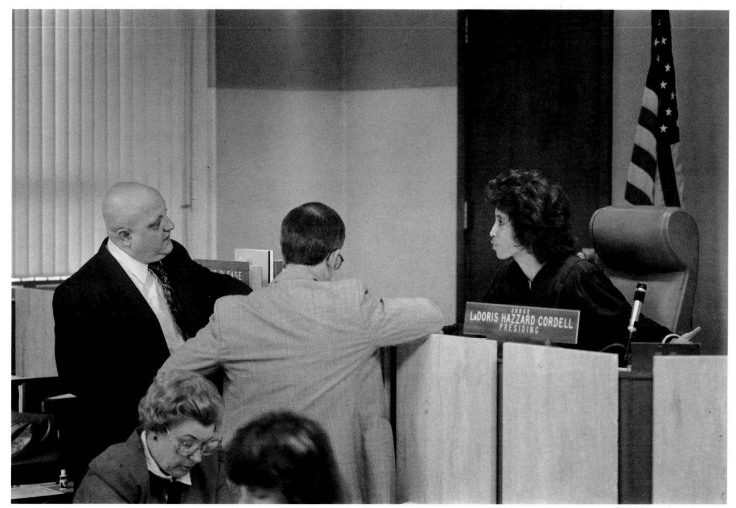

Douglas Robert Burrows

HOMEMAKER & MOTHER

Mary Demers, 30, begins her busy day at 6:30 a.m. and considers her primary job as mother and homemaker a 24-hour-a-day job. She is also working towards goals of having a fourth child and applying to a doctorate program at Stanford University in health psychology.

Basically, my life is centered around raising my family, graduate work, community work, exercise and shopping, in that order. I am a mother of three: Jennifer, age eight; Philip, age four; and Katie, age two. Often overlooked is the fact that moms have less consistency in their day due to interruptions in their own work by the kids throughout the day; constantly being relied on for answers to questions, for drinks and snacks, to cure the "I don't have anything to do" syndrome, to dry the tears as well as the laughter of daily events. The mental energy is often overwhelming when this is dealt with at three different age levels. A regimented schedule, like that of a working person, does not exist in the role of a mom. My schedule *must* stay flexible to the needs of the kids. To be a health care provider, educator, cook, cleaning lady, chauffer, and a security blanket of love — flexibility becomes the reality of motherhood.

Generally, my daily routine goes as follows:

6:30 a.m.: Get up, fix coffee as the neighbor ladies meet at my house. Four of us walk in the morning from 6:30 to 7:30.

7:30: Get Jenny, Philip, and Katie up, dressed, and fed. Make lunches.

8:30: Carpool nine kids to two different schools.

9:00: Work in library at St. Martin's school — reading appreciation with the second grade.

9:40: Go home. Take a coffee break and get dressed for aerobics.

10:00: Meet the girls at aerobics class.

11:00: Run errands, go shopping.

12:00 p.m.: Carpool pickup at preschool.

12:30: Lunch

1:00: Put Katie down for a nap. Garden awhile, read until 2:30.

2:30: Carpool to St. Martin's and drop darlings off at various houses.

3:00: Go home. Get Jenny dressed for Brownies (Mondays), soccer (Tuesdays and Thursdays).

3:30: Pick Philip up at friends (Monday/Wednesday); take home friend (Tuesday/Thursday). Carpool Jenny to after-school activity.

4:00: Get dinner started.

5:00: Dinner's served.

5:45: Baths for kids.

6:30: Classes at Santa Clara University (Monday/Wednesday) Meetings for various committees:
• Parish Finance Committee;
• Annual Diocese Appeal;
• Nursery (Chairwoman);
• Parish Council (will run for President elect)

10:00: Home . . . have a glass of wine. Read the paper and watch the news with Phil.

11:30: Phil and I read for 15 minutes to each other every night (it always seems to be my turn) .

12:00 a.m.: Lights out .

3:30: Lights on — Katie has had a bad dream. I bring her into bed with us . . . lights out.

Photos: Martha Jane Stanton

IRON WORKER

Patsy L. Davis, 38, is an Iron Worker who hopes that when her grand-daughter grows up, women on a construction job will just be old hat.

At 5' 1½" tall and about 110 pounds, I am a rather petite looking grandmother who is also an apprentice iron worker. The work is heavy and hard on the body. It sure builds muscle up and I will have some pretty good muscles if I live through this program which lasts three years. I am still in my first year, but I've got to make it since I can't type!

An iron worker is a construction worker who puts up the iron, decking, steel stairs, handrails and the all around structural steel in bridges, hotels, high-rises, whatever. We do about all the fabrication of the metal that goes into a building and almost all of the welding that holds the place together. As an iron worker, I have to be able to read many types of blueprints. We also put together the big cranes that do the heavy lifting on construction sites along with the rigging; moving large equipment in and around a building; and setting the steel that is the backbone of any large building. It's not unusual to be working 20 stories up on a building that will top out at 32 floors.

I've always wanted to travel and construction workers do travel with the jobs. I never had the chance to reach out into fields that may cause one to travel before now, because I was raising my children. Now with one married and the other living with his father, I can reach out. I got the chance to get into an iron workers' program and took it. I get paid while I learn on the job. I'm rather old for an apprentice and this does cause problems with the attitude of some I have to work with. My size and sex also cause some of the men to expect me not to be able to do my part. Their attitude does cause me anxiety at times, but on the whole, I've found that most of the men will give a woman a chance if she shows she really wants to learn and do her work.

I feel a woman has the right to earn a good wage as much as a man. She has to really work for the chance in construction. You have to give it your all. The work is heavy. The weather is either hot or cold and the hours can be very long. The strong language used by the men has to be over looked. After all, most of these guys have been at this work for years and have always talked like that, and just because a woman wants to try the work doesn't give her the right to dictate how a man talks. As long as the words are not aimed at me, I just shut them out.

The work can be very hard and I pray that I have the willpower to hold on 'til I can become a really good iron worker. By the time my grandchild grows up, I hope that women on a construction job will be just old hat. After all, she may very well want to be one of the iron workers one day.

Kathleen Smith-Barry

WAITRESS

Sandra Ann Taylor, 36, is Head Waitress at a delicatessen.

I was born and raised in New Jersey and I have always worked because it made me feel independent. For instance, I started working at the age of eight shining doorknobs, so I never had to ask anybody for money and I felt the freedom of being what I pleased. I had many odd jobs after that.

After high school, I went into office work for about six years, but I got tired of sitting at a desk. On my lunch hour I would go to a restaurant where my friend worked as a waitress. The place was always busy, so I would help her serve the food. I really loved it and thought it was fun because I am an energetic person. Of course, my friend thought I was crazy.

I decided to become a waitress, so I picked my favorite restaurant and was determined to get a job there. I did, and ended up working there for three years. Then I moved to Los Angeles and started working in a delicatessen because it had a faster pace and I like it better than a dinner house. Another reason why I liked waitressing was because I wanted to make people's meals more enjoyable.

Presently, I am the head waitress, which means I'm in charge of hiring, scheduling, training and making sure things run smoothly. Things don't always run smoothly though. People take their problems out on a waitress, but I really feel sorry for them — they don't even know how to control themselves. Also, when business is bad in a restaurant, it's always the waitresses' fault, but when business is good, they have nothing to do with it. And that's the truth.

But what really bothers me the most is that people sometimes have this attitude of "oh you poor thing you — having to work on a Saturday night . . . ." But this is the work I have chosen. That's why I carry myself the way I do. I take a lot of pride in myself and in my work, which is why I'm very good at what I do.

Presently, I am taking classes in career development to help me discover what my next venture in the working world will be.

Beth Herzhaft

WEAVER

Melitta Városy, 44, is a weaver working out of her own studio.

In the mid-70s as my marriage was dissolving, I was faced with the age-old dilemma of how to make a living, and stay home to be available as a full-time mother. The answer came from my loom. I turned the passion for weaving into a job, my garage into a production studio, and my kids grew up with a healthy perspective on what moms do, and a firsthand experience with work being part of life. Ten years and two additional floor looms later, I am still weaving wall hangings on a contract basis for the same manufacturer.

I suppose the best part of this job has been the indirect benefits it provides — there certainly isn't much money in it. Working with your hands doesn't seem to be a highly valued endeavor in America. Textile mills, steel towns, family farms are fading into extinction. But the relative freedom and independence I have as a self-employed production weaver means I can live where and how I want, work at home, create my own workplace, set my own schedule. These challenges I really enjoy. I have also been able to stay very involved in my kids' educational process; include them in my workplace; and teach them and some of their friends the almost forgotten skills of a weaving studio.

As my value system and priorities became harder and harder to maintain against the onslaught of the abstract religion of progress, an opportunity to move to a rural area of California became very attractive. Since I could take my job with me, the kids and I just packed everything — household and studio — and moved to a small town in the Sierra foothills. A small, old barn became the new studio. We all learned to cut our own firewood, tend the woodstove all winter, and the strawberry and corn patch in the summer. There have been prices to pay; long distance friendships are difficult to maintain. Life in small-town, rural America is cheaper, simpler and more down-to-earth, but also less exciting and stimulating, more work, and folks are often more narrow-minded. The customary one-hour violin lesson became an all day trip to the city. Same with concerts, good films, Italian shoes and espresso.

All in all, it has been a wonderful, if sometimes scary adventure. With my kids off on their own life adventures now at a university and music conservatory, I am entering on a new and different creative phase of my life. I am able to spend more time on designing and experimenting. Perhaps I'll organize my own cottage industry of handweavers. Maybe raise Angora goats.

Through all of this, we as a family learned some things:
Women and moms (and men) can, and do all kinds of work.
Blue skies, spring water, peace and quiet can be, and are, part of many people's everyday lives.
We don't need television.
You *can* make a living doing what you like.
It's worth listening (marching) to your own inner, "different drummer."
And finally, how important our hands, good friends, deer, oak trees, hawks and great blue heron are in our lives.

George Brich

RANCHER

Sharon Jo Stucky Edsall, 29, is a rancher who works with her husband.

Born in Bozeman, Montana, I'm the second of five children. When I was born, my parents were buying the Stucky family ranch which had been in our family for three generations. My mother worked at the college in Bozeman on and off 'til I was ten. Besides running the ranch, my dad broke horses and took out hunters in the fall.

From the time I could walk I followed by dad and grandpa everywhere. I was a "tomboy" through and through. My main interest was horses, but everything that happened on the ranch was a concern of mine. I started roping before I was ten years old, and just doing it all the time whenever I could. I liked working with the animals, it gets in your blood. By the time I was a senior in high school, I qualified for the National Finals in breakaway roping.

When I was ten my dad took a job on the Flying D Ranch which was about 150,000 acres at the time and his job was to oversee the cowboy crew which rode full time, year around, doing everything from calving to weaning to shipping. Girls just didn't get to go with the crew very often, but because I was my dad's daughter, I got to go. And I went every chance I could get. I was on a horse from the time I was four or five years old and felt very privileged. I got to do things such as rope calves when we branded and help during calving and trail cows. But there were no women on the crew, and never were until just a few years ago, and it was only a couple of wives that did.

I met my husband, Merle, at the Flying D when my dad hired him. I knew him for a couple of years, and when I was 18 he asked me out. After we went together for a year, we married. Now, Merle and I are leasing a ranch, but it is our dream to own a ranch. When you raise a good calf crop and do things right, and it's yours, there's no better feeling. You can be proud of someone else's cattle or horses, but I'm a lot more satisfied if they are my own. Sometimes it's a lot worse because you work so hard, fighting an uphill battle, but it's worth it in the end. Right now, times are really tough in the cattle industry. You have to cut corners whenever and wherever you can.

This life is great! It's what I really want to do, but I don't want to lead you into thinking it's all fun and glory. It's a business just like any other — you have to make a living. Sometimes when we lose two or three calves, cripple our horse, the tractor breaks down or we have cows with sunburned tits, I wonder where it's all going to end. Sometimes it would be nice to quit at 5 p.m. It just all adds up and I'm completely worn out. It's also hard to work outside most of the day and cook, keep house and take care of my two boys. The house is what usually gets left. It always waits for me.

Merle and I each have separate chores, but most of the time we work together. It's both of us together, down the line. We kind of check with each other: "I think that calf is sick, what do you think?" It's a two-way street. I would like to do more riding, just stay with the cows, but I still have the house and kids, and there is always haying in the summer that no one really likes, but it has to be done. You take the good with the bad, and you just hope there is enough good.

Orah Moore

SENIOR CITIZEN COORDINATOR

Maude Callen, 86, is manager of the Senior Citizens Nutrition Site in Pineville, South Carolina, where she serves some 50 elderly residents meals five days a week as well as delivering homebound meals in the countryside. "Miss Maude," as she is referred to by acquaintances, says, "I am working for senior citizens, I'm one myself, and I take care of everything that pertains to the elderly. I'm crazy about my work, I can help those who can't help themselves. That's the way I help myself."

Most of her life Miss Maude has been busy helping others, primarily as a nurse, health educator and midwife, working with the poor in rural Berkeley County, South Carolina. She first came to this area in 1923 as a missionary nurse for the Episcopalian Church, teaching local women how to become midwives, giving inoculations at schools and caring for the sick. She established the first venereal disease clinic and the first pre-natal clinic in the county. "When I came up here, there wasn't a paved road in this area," recalls Miss Maude. "There were no telephones or electric lights. There was no hospital. They were giving me $80 a month, and it took me three years before I could buy a new car, paying $12 a month."

Miss Maude's grandmother was a midwife in Florida, and she remembers that when her grandmother was working she "went around with a basket and for a long time I thought children came out of the creek." Orphaned at seven, Miss Maude was raised by an uncle in Tallahassee, Florida who was a doctor. She graduated from Florida A&M College, and later, the Georgia Infirmary in Savannah. After marrying, Miss Maude moved to South Carolina and eventually studied obstetrics at Tuskegee, becoming a Certified Nurse Midwife. Her work in public health was documented for "Life" magazine in 1951 in a photographic essay by W. Eugene Smith. As a result of the exposure in "Life," the public responded with some $25,000 in donations, making it possible for her to build the Maude E. Callen Clinic, the first in the county and the present location of the Senior Citizens Nutrition Site.

She has been honored with numerous awards, and has traveled to Washington, D.C. and New York to attend meetings on aging. In the spring of 1986 she got a call from the White House requesting her presence the following day to receive an award from the President. Her response: "I told them, I've got people to feed, and I have personal things to do. You just tell President Reagan I certainly don't have a hairdresser like Nancy and don't call me today and ask me to be in Washington tomorrow." She adds for emphasis, "The Johnny Carson Show called me the same way, at the last minute, and I told them the same thing."

After retiring from her public health work in 1977, Miss Maude began volunteering her time working with senior citizens, many of them younger than her. Her days continue to be full — with work and laughter — and she often drives some 40 miles a day to deliver meals to housebound seniors. When asked if she feels 86, she responds, "I don't know . . . how are you supposed to feel when you're 86?"

BOATYARD WORKER

Camilla Bratenahl Biller, 33, is supervisor of a boatyard and an avid sailor who has sailed the West coast numerous times as well as to Hawaii and the Galápagos Islands.

I was taught to work on boats by my father from the age of six. Both my parents encouraged me to sail and spend time in and around boats. I spent my summers as a child and full-time as an adolescent in a small rural town on a beautiful bay in Northern California. Everyone I know was involved with boats in one way or another, and it was natural for me to work on boats as a source of teenage income as well as use boats for recreation.

As soon as I got tired of living off odd jobs, I moved to the Bay Area in search of work. Naturally, I applied for a job at a boatyard in Sausalito, but got laughed out of the place. That experience set me back a little, so I turned to working as a sailmaker. It was easy to get a job as a seamstress, but I knew I did not want to do that very long because it did not pay very well and I wanted to spend more time outdoors. I soon graduated to cover maker which lasted three years.

By this time, I had some money saved up and needed a place to live, so I looked for a boat to buy. I bought a 31-foot, Norwegian wooden cutter that needed a lot of work. I had been racing aboard the boat of a friend who worked at the boat works shop where I now work. Lee, who is more skilled than anyone I know, took me under his wing and helped me begin to restore my boat. I was able to complete several major projects on my boat and the boatyard was favorably impressed, which eventually led to my job in 1972.

The owner of the yard saw that I had tools and the knowledge to use them and asked me if I wanted a job. The biggest objection I heard when I was hired was that the men would have to shut the bathroom door from then on. That was 12 years ago. They were then, and are now, the best group of people anyone could ask for. I sometimes get quizzical looks and occasionally even resentment from the customers. They just don't expect to see me there running the yard. With most customers, I am able to develop a wonderful rapport, and enjoy seeing them on their annual visit.

I am married and my husband is also a boatyard manager. Our boat is still being rebuilt, but fortunately, the pace has quickened. We salmon fish in the ocean all the time, and are planning a trip to my home bay this summer. I have sailed extensively up and down the West coast and Mexico, and to Hawaii and the Galápagos. Every trip was exciting and fun. I will be very happy when our boat will be finished enough to make our own trips and not on someone else's itinerary.

My job is satisfying and challenging in that I am able to give very legitimate advice and assistance to a talented group of co-workers, all men, some of whom are quite a bit older than me. It satisfies my requirements of being outdoors and near the water, but perhaps I will try something else. I am studying to get an ocean operator's license and possibly run a charter fishing boat.

Ann Meredith

LAWYER

Abby Abinanti, 38, has her own law practice and specializes in Indian law.

There came a time when I agreed to it, but I never really wanted to be a lawyer. In 1970 when I was graduating from college, the Bureau of Indian Affairs announced a scholarship program. Nationally at that time only a handful of Indian people had become lawyers, and many of them were not in their work "Indian" identified. The importance of lawyers to my community was emphasized to me by older women who understood our increasing need to look to the courts to protect our rights against encroachment — hunting, fishing, territorial, etc. and to enforce promises given at an earlier time when the "value" of those promises was not "understood." They wanted Indian lawyers for the fight. I was one of the few people graduating from our area, and since a college degree was a prerequisite to law school, I was elected. I agreed, because in fact there appeared to be, in the face of their insistence, no good reason not to go.

After graduating from college, I went off to a summer session for Indians designed to prepare us for law school. Unfortunately, no one prepared the law schools for us. After summering in a very supportive academic program we returned to our respective home states to begin law school. In my school one other Indian was enrolled, some people had two or three. I, along with my two best friends from summer school in two different states, was asked to leave the law school of my choice after the first year. They cited a combination of academic and "attitude" problems. They didn't like us not being like them and we didn't like them not liking us for not being like them. Not a good combination. For myself, I realize now from this distance a little coalition building might have prevented some of my anguish, but I had yet to discover that art form. Instead, I returned to the University of New Mexico's School of Law which admitted me in my second year. I finished at New Mexico, supported by an administration who believed Indian people should have Indian lawyers and who weren't offended by my not fitting the image of a law student.

In all of these years there has been trouble, people did not like or accept the idea of Indians or women being lawyers. Some people could not decide which idea they hated more. Some pretended that it didn't make any difference, that we were all the same. I, too, could be "one of the boys," "one of the white boys." Not likely. Both of those approaches created problems for me. These problems were overlayed by the gap in my experience/reality that, though I was technically a "lawyer," law school actually had not made me into a working lawyer. In recent years, I have become a lawyer, and become more of one everyday. I have helped; I have made a difference, a couple of times in a big way, mostly in a small way. I have learned that I have a role that includes being responsible for provision of legal services, not being a leader. I am part of a community, a culture which needs me to do my job, and that other people will do theirs and a whole will be created.

Personally, my years of being a lawyer have been troubled until recently. I have made terrible mistakes; offended people, friends; done things in a wrong manner; said words and acted in ways I can never take back, all of which hurt people. Much of this I will regret the rest of my life. At about the time I became a lawyer I began my personal struggle with the disease of alcoholism, the drinking, the co-dependency, the syndrome of the "adult child of an alcoholic." It has spanned all of these years. But it has been only in the last couple of years that we learned to reach out, to form coalitions, friendships that would give me the peace and the strength to act as an Indian person — to respect other humans, Indian and non-Indians. To respect people on their terms, not just on mine.

As for being a lawyer, I am at peace with that now. I just want to be able not so much to help Indian people, but to empower them to do for themselves. This is different than what I started out to do. I wanted to do great things. Now I just want to do a good job. For myself, I want to stay clean and sober and have the thrill of seeing the culture become clean and sober; watch as we regain and reclaim our full strength and independence.

Nita Winter

FARMERS

Diane Bowman-Friend, 29, and her sister, Barbara Bowman, 27, work together running the family farm.

I have always loved working on the ranch, even though at times it drained me mentally and physically. My first years farming were interesting from the standpoint of "local community acceptance." Ironically, the worst opposition I had came from the local women (farmers' wives) rather than from the local men (neighboring farmers). I found myself really going out to these women, trying not to alienate them from me. Their acceptance was important in order to break down the barriers between the sexes. I feel that their daughters would not have an opportunity to do what I'm doing if their mothers portrayed me negatively.

I remember looking and searching for role models when I was young and at that time, there weren't many who chose careers in untraditional fields. My sister and I are fortunate that we were encouraged by our parents to get involved with the farm. There are six girls in our family, no boys, and I suspect that had something to do with Dad's encouragement. Quite possibly, a son would have gotten all my Dad's attention. Nevertheless, support and encouragement motivate people into areas they might not otherwise pursue.

Barbara and I have worked together all of our lives, but most seriously for the past two years. It's funny being adults now, working as colleagues, yet still enjoying the sibling friendship. We're very different from one another in some ways, such as personality, disposition and opinions; but we have one common bond and that's this ranch. We feel an attachment to the land our Dad spent years building up and feel a certain amount of responsibility to continue the operation successfully. The economics of farming have been lagging these past few years, but we're motivated by the future and what it holds."

Diane

The most difficult part of working on the farm is when I can't do something . . . usually it's something that's either physically demanding or technical. I force myself to try, try harder to find a solution without running for my sister or one of the men to help me. It's not a matter of pride that stops me, it's a matter of accomplishing something on my own. I think women have a tendency to "give up" instead of pushing themselves to stretch the limits of their minds and bodies. I know I do, but if I'm going to be a successful farmer, I must compete with myself to attain greater self confidence.

We are all conditioned through our adolescence to be "careful" or "don't worry, daddy will take care of you" or to "marry a nice man to support you." But as an adult woman now, I want to face the world and its problems on my own, using whatever technique it takes to find solutions. I've found various solutions to the same problem, just by thinking creatively. The men I work with didn't understand my motives at first. They perceived my trying to impress them. After lots of dialogue of honest, heart-to-heart talks, we did come to a better understanding of me, them, and the issues that face women/men working relationships.

Barbara

Pam Benham

BALLOON FACTORY WORKER

Rose M. Coburn, 53, works at a rubber company as a balloon stripper.

Born and raised on a 200-acre farm here in Atwater, Ohio, I always worked in the fields with my father, and helped with the cows, chickens and pigs. Even after graduation from high school I preferred this type of work to an inside job. My father needed help, anyway. However, I knew that I would have to get a job sometime. I was a *very* shy girl, but in 1959 I went to Chicago where a friend got me a job in an exclusive flower and gift shop making $1.50 an hour. I became their head packer and gift wrapper in both the flower shop and gift shop, which sold a lot of fine china, crystal and silver.

It was a nice enough job, and I gained much experience and made many good friends — many of whom I still hear from — however, this farm girl was never really content in the big city. My parents were getting up in years and I felt my father could use the help back on the farm. So, after five years I came back to Ohio. On Saturday evening after work at the flower shop, I took off without telling my fellow employees, but I found out later they knew I was leaving. I arrived early Sunday morning back home and started working at the rubber company on Monday morning. Little did I know what I was getting into!

Although I have worked in several different departments, most of the time has been spent stripping balloons on the automatic balloon machine. Although it may look easy to a bystander, it is really a very hard job. It wasn't so bad several years back, but like everywhere else, I guess, production was speeded up and quality lowered. Materials were cheapened and so was the finished product. And no one seems to care. I used to be able to take pride in my work, but anymore I am almost ashamed to admit I had any part in its production. There have been times when the factory has gone to other areas because there was cheaper labor — meaning they didn't have strong unions and offered fewer benefits.

It isn't really what I would call gratifying work. It is just a job. Many trainees never make it, and many others have trouble with their hands and arms working the balloons on and off the forms, which results in much sick leave. I work seven-and-a-half hours a day and I'm on my feet practically the whole time. Sometimes my legs and feet hurt so bad I can't hardly stand up when I get home. The shop can get very hot at times, maybe up to a 100 degrees and they don't have an air conditioner. All they have is an air maker which draws the hot air inside, and fans that blow in my face all day. I started at the balloon factory 22 years ago at $1.31 an hour, and right now I'm making $6.91 an hour. I lived at home with my parents and I didn't have that many expenses on my own, but for a family it would be hard. Most of the other girls I work with feel the same way I do, but a lot of them have husbands who are out of work.

I'm still just a farm girl at heart. Even though my parents sold the farm, just keeping two acres several years back, and they are both recently deceased, I still have some chickens, calves, cats, a big garden and an acre of corn that I plant for my calves. The women at work say that since my mother died I should get out and do this and that. But I say that's not me, I'm content in my little corner. When I retire I'd be happy to stay with my flowers and vegetable garden and animals . . . that would be all right with me.

William D. Wade

DOG GROOMER & BELLY DANCER

Suzi Thompson, 33, runs her own dog grooming business during the day and works part-time as a belly dancer nights.

When I was fourteen I had to write a term paper for English class and the only books I could find that interested me enough to write about were about dogs. Ironically, at the same time I was given a border collie that I fell madly in love with. We went to obedience school and did so well that we started competing in trials at AKC dog shows. When I graduated from school I wanted to learn how to train protection and guard dogs. However, I had worked for four years at a fast food restaurant to save money to learn a skill, but it still wasn't enough to go to training school. So, I settled for a dog grooming school instead. I attended the Chicago branch of the New York School of Dog Grooming and graduated three months later from the shop owner's course.

Then I bounced around Chicago for awhile working and experiencing life. Finally, I returned to Illinois and opened a grooming business at a kennel that had just opened. I held down a second job as a cocktail waitress at night. I was worn out from working at the kennel from 8 a.m. until 6 p.m. and then the nightclub from 8 p.m. to 4 a.m. My health was deteriorating so, money or no money, I quit the night job. Then, to get back into shape I started studying kung fu. I worked out five nights a week, three or four hours a night, and loved it. You have to combine mental and physical effort and concentration in order to achieve your goals. Eight months later I decided to combine mental and physical abilities, but have fun with it doing something different — belly dancing. It basically employs the same training as the martial arts. Control, balance, concentration, relaxation, strength, agility, and energy flow are just some of the comparisons. Well, the kung fu school closed, but I kept on dancing.

In the meantime, I ended a nine-year relationship with a bang. I was pregnant and already knew after nine years that I could not possibly marry the father. We would just end up divorced. I asked him for help in my eighth month of pregnancy because I had to give up my job. He informed me that he would not help me with the doctor or hospital bill unless I married him. I just couldn't do it, so I turned to my mother for help and she supported me for a short time until I was back on my feet.

With a child to take care of, I opened another dog grooming business at home and called it Artistic Canine Grooming. I worked as much as I could with a baby to take care of, though it wasn't easy. The father never has paid child support or anything. When my daughter was two years old, I had an opportunity to move to Arizona and perform in nice restaurants and nightclubs. However, I decided it wouldn't be good for my little girl, so I stayed put and groomed full-time and danced part-time at ethnic festivals, birthday parties, etcetera.

My daughter is ten years old now and very happy. I never have married because I've never met anyone as yet that I wanted to marry. I support my family totally on what I earn. By the time I pay the expenses and taxes I owe, I end up working very long hours. I would say that dog grooming is equally open to men and women. As for that matter, so is belly dancing. One of the very best instructors I've had in Middle Eastern dance is a man. And all of my instructors at dog grooming school were men. The most difficult part of my life is finances. I work very hard, long hours, but being independent has a price. Who knows, maybe I'll win the lottery!

I do feel I have my priorities in order. God blessed me with a precious, beautiful daughter to raise and love and that's what I'm doing. In the meantime, I'll keep working on my finances and getting myself together. Recently, I joined a new karate school! I do enjoy my work and I adore the dogs I work with as I usually see them often, and I am very close to them. And I love to make people happy when I dance; I love performing. For me, belly dancing, like dog grooming, is my outlet for creative expression.

Photos: Linda Smogor

SUGAR CANE HARVESTER

Clarita Berroga Suniga, 35, has been working in the sugar cane fields on the Hawaiian island of Kauai for the past 12 years. Originally from the Philippines, she moved to Hawaii with her husband in 1971, and they have three children, ages 13, nine and five. Suniga spoke about her life and work in simple terms since English is a second language for her.

When I came to Hawaii, I could speak only a little English. I learned by hearing, but not that much. My children help me, they correct my English. I am sorry for my English. I didn't go to college, not even high school . . . I only go to the sixth grade in the Philippines. After that, I worked on the farm with my parents. I grow rice, corn, tomatoes, eggplant, and I sell these things at the market.

I had to find money, that's why I left the Philippines. In Hawaii, I worked at a pineapple cannery, but not too long, about six months, then they closed the company. I got a job at the Lihue Plantation and they showed me how to work in the fields. I start work at seven in the morning and work until 3:30; I cut the cane and lay it out. A tempered knife cuts the cane real easy, but my hands get tired from cutting the cane all day, and sometimes they get numb. I rub them with alcohol, that helps.

I like the job, it's not so hard. The only thing, it's hot and makes me tired. I wear coveralls and long sleeves. Other jobs at the company are planting, irrigation, harvesting, factory work. I want to stay in the fields . . . it's the job I can do, I know how to do it. I'm happy with my job.

I like Hawaii, it's better than the Philippines. It was hard to find money there. I make $7.31 an hour, and 12 years ago I got four dollars an hour. My husband works for the same company as a truck driver. Now, we have a house in Lihue and we have a car. My children, I tell them to study more so they don't do work like I do. I want them to go to college.

Ann Meredith

SCIENCE COORDINATOR

Cheryl M. Hawthorne, 27, is a physical science coordinator at the Lawrence Hall of Science at the University of California Berkeley.

As a physical science coordinator, I develop and teach physics, chemistry, biology, and geology as well as robotics to elementary and high school students, which I have been doing for the past eight years. Even though I have always enjoyed playing school, tutoring and teaching my friends, I never planned on being a teacher. My career goals in high school were to attend medical or pharmacology school.

When I graduated from high school, I got a job in a summer engineering training program for four years. With each new job assignment, I was faced with new supervisors and their prejudices. All of my supervisors were men and they all had the tendency to give me secretarial and clerical tasks to perform. It was there that I realized how chauvinistic men are towards women in science. Each time I would remind my supervisor that I was an engineering student with the ability to calculate, design, draft and solve problems. I fought them every step of the way and demanded they teach me the engineering skills that I was hired to learn. As long as I reminded them of this, I was given challenging tasks to perform in order to learn engineering techniques. It was this opposition and attitude that gave me the drive to compete with these men and to prove that a woman's place is anywhere she chooses it to be.

I attended Stanford University in 1977 as a pre-med student, but after one year my parents and I decided that the tuition was too much of a burden on all of us. So, I applied to UC Berkeley in the field of civil engineering because I was told there was a better chance of being accepted in this field since there were fewer people enrolling. I found it very hard to keep up with the physics, computer science and calculus classes during my first quarter in civil engineering. I transferred into the College of Letters and Sciences at the end of the year. With the array of physics, chemistry, biology, computer science and calculus courses that I had taken, it only made sense to pursue a degree in physical sciences. I finally graduated with a bachelor's degree in physical science in 1983.

Since then, I have started my own business, taking science programs into low income areas during my off hours at Lawrence Hall. I really like working independently and developing the classes that I want to teach through my own company. I do have some freedom on the job, but I still have other people that I must consult with on my development projects.

Many people are surprised at the amount of independence, recognition and respect that I receive, especially being black and female. I must admit, I have never been confronted with racist attitudes or statements on my job, and I have never been treated with anything but respect. The funny thing, however, is that I'm the only black in my department and I always have been. There has never been another black staff person hired in the eight years I've been there, which is a nice slap in the face if I look at myself as the "token nigger." I try not to think of things that way. I hope that I'm respected because of the good work I do and the raving reviews I receive; this is the way I'd prefer to look at things. My parents taught me never to "cry prejudice" when something goes wrong. My brother, sister and I were always taught to overlook what may seem like prejudice and work extra hard at the job to make others overlook our skin color. This has worked very well for me.

My home training and family support is very much responsible for my present success. My parents have taught me to never give up. They have helped me love school and learning along with independence, self-respect, strength and endurance.

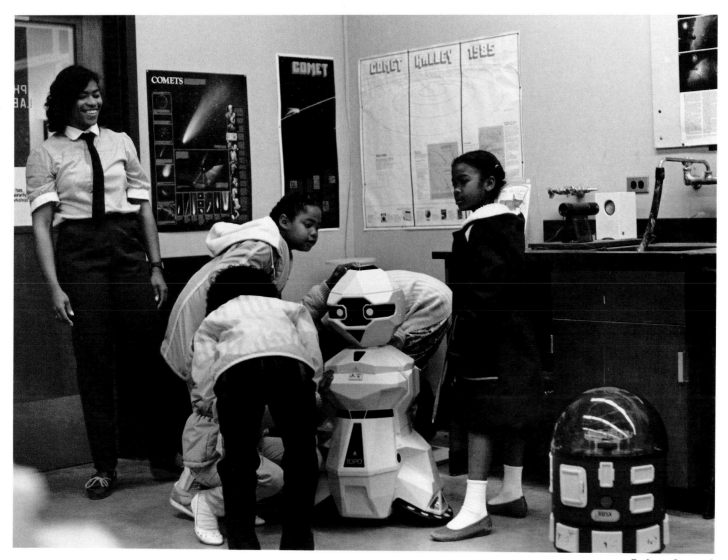

Ruthann Stenmark

COSTUME DESIGNER

Kelly Kimball, 46, is a costume designer for the entertainment industry. Her work includes costumes for the feature film, "Clan of the Cave Bear" and Michael Jackson's "Thriller."

I have been an artist since I was born; I never considered anything else. I grew up in a family of artists, went to art school, married a painter, and now my daughter is in art school. I never thought much about what my specific career in art would be, so when I entered the job market rather abruptly with a divorce, desperate for money, I took the first job I could get. It lasted as long as the company did . . . a few months. That was the first and last non-art related job I ever had.

When I began to work, there were no services to help the single working mother. For awhile, I was teaching art to children, and I was surrounded by women with young children. Just knowing this gives you a feeling of support, real or imagined. But then when I entered the costuming field, I met very few young women my age with children. Working in this industry is demanding; there are long hours, and sometimes months at a location distant from home. (Recently, one young vice president of a large studio, who thought of himself as an "innovator," balked at the suggestion of putting in a childcare facility on the lot.) The part my daughter says she hated the most was when I had a steady job in television and she was going through adolescence. I sometimes had to work overtime and on Saturdays, and she says the hours spent alone were the worst. That's when she began to have trouble and started cutting school. It just didn't work out.

The most often asked questions are, "How does one break into the entertainment industry?", or "How did *you* get into this business?" Well, there are as many answers as there are people working. You just have to make your own way. I just happened to hear of a costume shop that was trying to finish a lot of work for "Disney on Parade." They had a deadline to meet, and needed some extra hands who could handle a variety of craft-related tasks. My art school background suited the job perfectly. When I walked into work that first day, I asked the boss to give me something messy to do so I wouldn't be expected to sew, as sewing is not one of my better talents — something my daughter thinks is very funny.

Aside from being seductive, the entertainment industry has proven helpful to me in ways other than financial. It feeds my own artwork at home with visual stimulation and ideas. My work with special-effects costuming brings me into contact with other craftsmen in the industry where there is a rich source of materials and methods. My interests outside the industry, in turn, feed the job.

Although I entered a field that is not typically thought of as a male-dominated community, my area is special effects or character costumes, which means that the assembly is more of a heavy duty construction than sewing. Because the construction involves a sometimes messy and rough procedure, these jobs are likely to be handed to men because they "know how to use tools." Well, nobody seemed to care if I was one of the ones there to do it. It was mostly things like "here, cut this on the band saw, do you think you can handle it?" And if I couldn't, then someone would simply show me how. Later on, when I ran my own department, people were just amazed that someone could build a six-foot taco costume at all, and not that a "girl" did it.

The work is not constant. When I finish a film, I never know when my next job will come. It can be a tense time. Sometimes I am out of work even as long as a year. But I have been living this way for a long time, supporting myself and daughter. I don't know how I've been doing it, but I have. I'm not sure that I would be happier in a more secure occupation.

George Brich

CONSTRUCTION EQUIPMENT OPERATOR

Joyce Shon, 37, has been a heavy equipment operator for public works for the past 12 years.

To go all the way back, I got into this line of work as an equipment operator by the accident of being the second child and the second daughter. Big sister was already apprenticed with Mom in the (then) acceptable arts of household management. Therefore, when I (my first big failure!) proved not to be the expected son, I became Dad's #1 assistant. And there was lots to do in a new house on a tight budget. To be fair, everybody helped with everything. We built retaining walls, landscaped, put in watering systems, poured concrete patios and paths, and kept the old Plymouth station wagon running. In those cold-war days, we even built a fallout shelter! With such a variety of activities as a child, it's not unusual that I never felt restricted to "traditional."

The public works field was not easy to get into on a career basis for a woman, but public awareness of women's rights at the time (1970's) definitely helped, and assistance from government agencies was available. I doubt I could have done it otherwise. Always, and still, there are difficulties on the daily work level, such as resistance from many men to the invasion of their territory. Being a very small minority of the work force makes you very obvious and subject to close scrutiny/criticism from skeptical co-workers. Men are people too, I remind myself. Some have been wonderful; patient, helpful, informative, supportive. And some have been dreadful, the archetypical macho-sexist type! With the latter, I eventually discovered that their hostility isn't necessarily personal, it seems consistently to stem from their own insecurities! I've refused to let their problems become mine — I like to feel good about myself! I've learned that a solid belief in my own competence is a necessary foundation to other people acknowledging it.

As an equipment operator, I am a very obvious part of a crew, both to co-workers and the public. One of the hardest things for me has been overcoming a fear of trying new techniques or equipment in front of an audience. No miracle cures or short cuts to offer here — just keep at it! I've seen so many women leave this field, overwhelmed by dealing with nonfamiliar work and outdated attitudes towards women. And worse, sorry to report, some women expect special privileges because they are women . . . well, women are people too! They make it harder for competent women to earn respect and recognition.

Some guidelines I developed for myself to survive: 1) Be conscientious about your work; 2) Be patient and persistent with yourself when learning new skills; 3) Be realistic about working in male territory — you're going to be hustled, harassed, unfairly criticized, and even sabotaged by an unpleasant minority. You're probably *not* going to change their attitudes and beliefs no matter how good you are! 4) Keep your self respect in good working order. 5) Most importantly, keep your sense of humor. There are going to be times when nothing else will keep you going — great advice from my mother. And then there are those pay-off times, a difficult job well done by group effort gives a sense of achievement and comraderie.

I've found the minor aggravations can get to me more than the major issues. I cancelled a subscription to a magazine that professed to address all the concerns of working mothers over a beauty column. First, there were endless covers of perfectly coiffed, dress-for-success moms with beribboned and ruffled daughters, *never* a pair of coveralls or hard hat. And then the ultimate insult — how to overcome the devastating effects of conditioned office air on complexion and hair. I nearly sent them a treatise on how to clean a face blackened with dust and diesel fumes; salvage a hairdo ravaged by long sweaty hours mashed under a hard hat; how to make stained and calloused hands presentable on a date; and just exactly what do you wear that won't call attention to the sunburned lines on your neck and arms.

I've been told that it's a "personal problem" that steel-toe-boots, gloves, rainwear, coveralls, and such *required* safety equipment are not provided in sizes to fit a 5'1" person with hips and breasts! But despite the problems, big and small, I like my job. I especially like the self-respect I've earned while overcoming obstacles and mastering skills.

Ann Meredith

HOSPITAL AIDE

Mary Ann Wiggins, 32, worked as a Hospital Aide for 10 years at a developmental center for the mentally retarded. After a divorce, she took time off to spend with her children. She is presently a Private Duty Nurse's Aide.

I started working at Apple Creek Developmental Center in 1974 when it was still called Apple Creek State Institution. Not only was there a change in name, but the place changed for the better. The change in the care of the residents who are mentally retarded, made a big change in some of the residents themselves. When I first worked there, one staff person would care for 15 to 20 residents. The only residents that attended school were those who were 18-years-old or younger. Soon after some big changes came about, Adult Education was developed. Then, all the residents attended school and grouped according to their ages. They even added a Geriatric Center.

I really enjoyed working there because it was a challenge. It gave me a chance to help where I was needed. It was fun, there were good times, and also bad times. There were some people you could help, and there were some you couldn't help, but just made them as comfortable as possible. It's not easy working at Apple Creek, it's a very emotional job because you deal with all types of residents as well as families. When I first started working at Apple Creek as a hospital aide, my duties included caring for patients —toileting, feeding, grooming and oral hygiene. Later on, I was a Therapeutic Program Worker which meant I did all the shopping for all the residents' needs or requests in rehab meetings. I also dealt with concerned parents, which I enjoyed. I traveled 30 miles each way, everyday, to get to my work.

The most important reason I left Apple Creek after ten years was for the rest. But also, I went through a divorce, leaving me with two children who are almost teenagers. We had a whole new adjustment to contend with. Being at Apple Creek itself sometimes caused emotionally depressing days. Plus, I was going through depressing times at home. Besides, my children and I needed to get to know each other again. It's hard being a mother and a father to teenage children, mentally and financially, but I enjoy it. Like Apple Creek, it's a challenge. But, through all my ups and downs, I did have my mother at my side, encouraging and praying for me, just being there for support. She also works at Apple Creek. Now, I've got my life together. My children are ready to take on life, I'm now working again as a Private Duty Nurse's Aide for the elderly, and I enjoy it. I have a new love in my life. I can honestly say I am a strong-willed working woman. Someday, I hope to be a Certified Nurse.

William D. Wade

POTTER

JoAnn Soge Track, 35, is an American Indian potter.

I feel that I have always had a choice as to where I want to be and what it is that I want to be doing. After graduation from high school, I attended the Institute of American Indian Arts where I studied writing, ceramics, theater and modern dance. After one-and-a-half years in Santa Fe, I very much wanted to travel, so I went to New York City, then on to Paris, France for the summer. The Louvre was fascinating, and I was astonished by the private collections of Native Art. While in France I saw as much as I could.

After the summer, I returned to New York City and stayed with friends. While in the city, I met a lot of Latinos, we talked about our lives and the struggle of native people. In 1971, I went to Cuba to help Fidel Castro in the sugar cane harvest. After two months of hard work and studies on Marxist/Leninist theory and socialism, I returned to New York City, and then to Taos Pueblo. Not being able to find a job, I went to the Navajo reservation and attended the Navajo community college.

After two years there, I returned to Taos Pueblo. After being away for some time, I realized the importance of our ancient styles, although I also had to allow my own creative needs to influence my work. I come from a family of artists, so I can't help but be inspired to work with the native clay from which we all come. My grandmother taught me how to respect our special clay and how to allow my spirit to emerge in the form of pottery. My grandmother worked in our pueblo's well known mica clay, and I am proud to carry on for my generation.

Scott Fields

SKYDIVING INSTRUCTOR

Virginia Morris, 21, is a skydiving instructor and Accelerated Free-fall Jumpmaster. She also is a full-time college student.

My skydiving interests started my first summer in college in 1983, after my two older brothers tried it and told me how much fun it was. While I could afford it, skydiving was a weekend hobby for me, but it became more expensive —that is, as I wanted to spend more and more money on it —I started working at the parachute school repacking parachutes. The money I made was enough so I could afford my own parachute as well as more jumps.

After about 300 jumps, my skydiving began to stagnate: I no longer felt challenged as I did when I was a novice. So, when I heard about a jumpmaster certification course at Perris Valley Airport in California, I signed up, hoping this would be the kind of challenge I needed to keep the sport exciting for me. The course was a one-week training camp, and all the participants were expert-licensed parachutists from all over the world. I must admit that the intensity of our assignments and evaluations intimidated me at first. I was the only woman in the class of 20 skydivers, but as with any group of people working together intently, we made friends and supported each other through the trials of bad weather, discouraging scores, and general uncertainty.

My job as an Accelerated Freefall (AFF) Jumpmaster consists of training novice parachutists in basic skydiving skills. I am certified to accompany the AFF students in freefall, along with another jumpmaster, when needed. This means that I grip the student's harness as he leaves the airplane. I contribute to his balanced descent in freefall, and I help make sure he accomplishes my planned maneuvers, especially a rip cord pull by a safe altitude. I carry a radio so I can talk my student down during his parachute flight and assist in making a safe landing on target. I am also responsible for evaluating the student's performance and progress and preparing him for the next level.

Although I've made over 500 skydives, I'm still new at this job, so I have not yet "seen it all," and I'm neither discouraged nor dis-illusioned about my work. In fact, it's very rewarding. I have always loved skydiving, so being able to "turn on" novices to my favorite

sport and watch them improve in freefall is something I get a big charge out of. I am meeting men and women from a wide variety of careers and age groups, but as long as they want to skydive, none of them are strangers to me. I suppose the most difficult part of my work is making my students understand the balance be-tween safety and fun in skydiving. That ranges from cancelling a jump because of high winds (unsafe conditions) to try-ing to calm a student's fears just prior to leaving the airplane at 12,500 feet. A student who is too cocky to be careful, is in as much risk as one who is too frightened to think straight. These are extreme examples, but they are the ones that try my patience and remind me that I really am an amateur psychologist, working through the anxieties of adults in a high-stress environment.

There's no *physical* reason that female skydiving instructors are so rarely seen. Today's gliding parachutes are lightweight to wear, they offer reliable openings and consistently soft landings, so the sport is not just for big, strong men. The best skydivers know that parachut-ing is not a "macho" sport, but a "mind over matter" sport. Because I'm a woman in a male-dominated sport, I meet hundreds of men, but to jump with the better skydivers I must still prove myself in the air as an alert, well-coordinated and "heads up" skydiver.

I plan to continue training skydivers indefinitely. After I graduate from college and settle into a career, I would like to compete in free-fall work as part of a four or eight-person fall team. Hopefully, my work as an instructor will help me afford to reach my goal to com-pete. I am also interested in being part of women's skydiving achievements such as the world record for the largest freefall forma-tion of women which now stands at 60. Due to the high level of self-reliance inherent in skydiving, I can go as far as I desire.

Photos: Mark Strayhorn

BAKER

Bette Shertzer, 41, is part of a collective bakery.

To talk about me and my work, I think I should start with where I am now, for I feel that I am not only doing "good" work, but work that is right for me. "On the Rise Bakery" in Syracuse, New York, is a collectively run, whole-grain bakery where everyone does everything, except the deliveries which we slowly but exhaustingly hired a friend to do. We bake breads, pastries and a few lunch items with all whole grains — wheat, corn, rye, etc. — and with as many organic, local and seasonal products as possible.

We see ourselves, now seven women, as creating an alternative way of thinking, working, being. We want people to see that it is possible to have *some* control over our lives; what we eat, how we work with one another and how we earn our livelihoods. Up until now, we have been mostly single women and, therefore, not "average wage-earners," but we are presently taking on women with families and are looking forward to the challenges this will present.

For me, this work is the culmination of many years of involvement in social change. I worked with food cooperatives and protest movements in the 60s and 70s and then, as I spent time reflecting over "what went wrong," I came to see deeper connections between one's own inner self and one's work and how one should reflect the other. I felt I very much needed to be putting my ideas into practice to see how they held up in reality and to be working at a physical job using my whole body, not just my mind. I wanted work that "centered" me, challenged me, and at the same time, showed people that alternatives *do* exist and can succeed if we are committed to work hard and creatively with one another through many ups and downs.

This is my fifth year at the bakery and I'm not bored yet! I sometimes forget in the middle of a summer day, standing in front of three ovens with 120 loaves of bread to keep track of, why it is that I'm doing this work. But, invariably, someone will come along to thank us for existing, or to ask for a donation, or to drop off some goat's milk yogurt, and I am reminded once again, how grateful I am to be a part of a network of people trying to provide good food, good work and good community.

Jan Phillips

DENTIST

Jennifer L. Crandall, 27, owns her own dental practice.

Nearly everyday I hear the question, "What made you want to be a dentist?" And, nearly everytime I give an injection, my blood pressure takes a dash upward while I maintain an outward expression of ease and control to my patient. Often, during this time I wonder, "What in the hell am I doing this for?"

I'm the type of person who sets her mind to do something, or go somewhere, and overcomes all obstacles to get it done and be there. In high school I decided I would be a dentist. I could have a special skill no one could take away. I could have control of my time and my environment. Thus, it sounded like great freedom; I could go anywhere and use this skill to help others and I could choose where I wanted to live. Dentistry needs women doctors, and so does the public. Because of the demand and freedom, I made a beeline to become a dentist. I finished my college degree with three majors in three years and graduated from dental school and started my own practice at the age of 23.

There were obstacles to overcome: My mother telling me I'm crazy to want the headaches of my own business; my father telling me dental school is too expensive and he can't afford it (over $60,000 for three years of tuition alone); my college counselor telling me I'll never get accepted to dental school because I was too young, a woman, and because I come from an unstable background of divorced parents. In dental school, instructors certainly tried to create their own barriers by keeping a special eye on female academics and clinical performances in addition to receiving sarcastic comments from lab instructors such as, "See ladies, it's just like baking a cake." Other obstacles included the practice management instructors warning us of the over busyness problem in dentistry, gloom and doom, and the impossibility of hanging a sign and starting a practice.

How did I hurdle? I presented my college counselor six letters of acceptance to six dental schools; a Bachelor of Arts with three majors in three years; and a Phi Beta Kappa at that. Being fortunate to have received one of seven scholastic and financial scholarships from the State of Arizona to a graduate program and with additional financial support from my mother, I never had to ask my father for a dime. For the dental school clinical instructors with their special eyes, I made them scowl with envy because I made certain I had fun with my patients, something they failed to achieve in private practice, thus leaving many of them with their only alternative to teach. For the lab instructors who were grading my lab cases, I always asked them if they liked chocolate chip cookies as I batted my eyelashes, jokingly of course; the trick was not to take their offensiveness seriously. And, as for Mom and the doom and gloom practice management instructors, the key to success is to truly care. However, moms are always right; having your own business is a headache, some of the time.

I love being a dentist, but I border between like and hate wearing all the many other hats of employer, business person, collection person at times, lab person, janitor, receptionist, bill payer, equipment service person, and a victim for insurance salespeople, financial planners, stockbrokers, and charitable organizations. Dentistry is fun; it's arty, creative, cosmetic and with instant results. It's also extremely dynamic technologically. My work is challenging and demanding with new materials constantly arriving and new equipment and techniques. And, being with different types of people all day long and sharing their life transitions and growth over six-month periods is inspiring.

Having to numb someone is not fun and makes me give second thoughts to what I'm doing in life. But, after explaining thoroughly, showing, and letting the patient participate in their dental care, I constantly get expressed appreciation after the patient's treatment. I'm always surprised to get a "thank you." Everyone hates going to the dentist, and yet to get a "thank you," along with a referral are the most wonderful compliments a dentist could ever receive; it's what keeps me going despite needles and noisy drills.

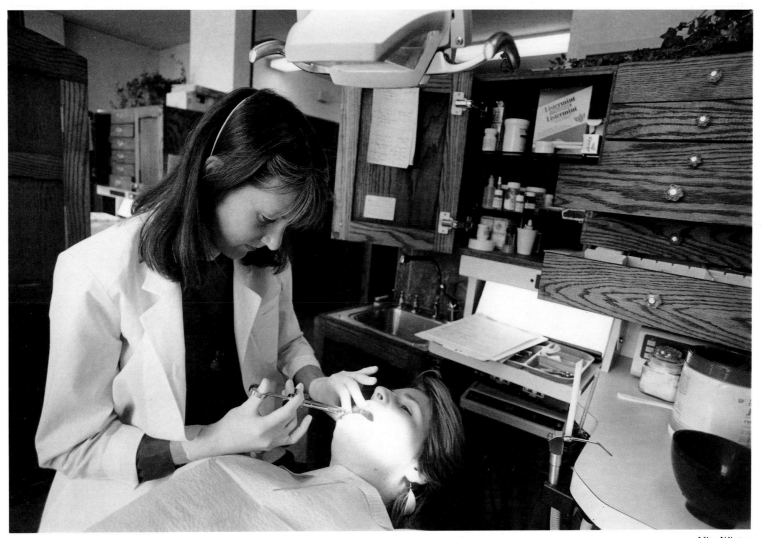

Nita Winter

CASHIER & LINE STOCKER

Lulú Castañeda, 31, first came to the United States from Mexico when she was 20 years old. She works in an egg packing plant to help support her two children and husband.

My hour to start at work is 5:30 a.m., so I get myself ready at 4:00 a.m. and prepare breakfast for my three children. Then, to begin my shift, I arrive at the egg packing plant and since supposedly I'm the one who speaks English the best, they assigned me to turn on the main machine. Every day I change the number on the computer which marks the boxes which will hold the eggs. The other day I realized that it is a privilege and all the workers on my shift depend on me. It happened that one day I ran out of gas in my car and I was delayed 17 minutes, and when I arrived at the packing plant my co-workers gave me an applause. Nobody had started their work because nobody has the knowledge to start the main machine and the computer. In spite of all, that gave my spirit a new lift. For the first time I felt important in my work.

After starting the main machine and the computer, I go to the line to inspect the eggs, selecting those which are first quality "AA" and separating those which are broken or "cracked." Every day I work one hour as a box girl, and on Wednesdays I work all day as a box girl which is the one day that I do not get dirty with egg. All other days, no matter how much I care for myself, my clothes get covered with egg, including my shoes, and to stand the horrible smell of egg on my clothes. My desperation is to get home before my children and my husband arrive from school and work to take a bath and prepare them dinner. And all this for $3.45 an hour.

In this country I feel like a pioneer because instead of living we survive like the immigrants that we are. Like many other people of different nationalities who have come to the United States in the past, we are all immigrants. Unfortunately, many have forgotten this. In the past, my Black brothers were treated like slaves, and Abraham Lincoln advocated in their behalf and liberated them. Kennedy was killed for the same principles of wanting to help minorities. Martin Luther King is today a hero. And who will advocate for us? How long will we be exploited and humiliated in this same land which belonged to our fathers? Only God knows. He is my hope. With much love to all the world, especially to the women who work in America.

Douglas Robert Burrows

MILLINER

Anthea Brown, 38, owns her own hat business, often juggling childcare for her two sons, with her work as a milliner.

I left my homeland, England, in 1974, and came to the United States, originally for a vacation, but we decided to stay. In England I had been an art teacher, but after a year, already felt institutionalized and depressed. Travel seemed the answer.

We found it difficult to get work in the U.S.A. without a greencard, and so after my husband found a job in the antique business, and I had a few false starts, I decided to start my own business and go it alone. How I chanced upon the idea of designing and making hats, I don't really know. It came as a flash of inspiration, after trying to think of something to do. Shortly afterwards, I opened my own hat shop in Venice, California. We were so poor that we lived in the back of the shop. We didn't have any babies right then, so it was alright. In fact, it was quite fun. Selling terrified me though.

A few months after I opened the shop, I took on a partner who was a friend. She made clothes, so we decided to combine our efforts. I had never made hats before, although I'd been trained in art and design, which was a good basis. I found time spent in the sculpture studio very useful. The American public was most tolerant of my efforts and I learned my craft on them. Americans seem to applaud a tryer. In England, we had this pinnacle of excellence constantly before us. It was both inspirational and oppressive. California was creatively very liberating.

Now, I have a studio in the building we call home and it's a much better life because I feel more in control than I was, and now our two sons aren't so small and can tolerate being ignored for an hour or so. But the part of me that is a designer lives in the same body as the mother, and they are not good friends. All too often, when it gets down to the crunch, the mother wins and the designer feels cheated. Simon, who is eight, and Oliver, who is six, will come into the workshop and sit down with me and draw. Then all the elements seem reconciled for a brief time. That is what I'm striving for, to tie all those parts of me together . . . to achieve autonomy.

You can maintain easily enough with children, but when you want to move ahead to accomplish something, the problems arise. Right now, I am working on a fashion show. Sometimes, I feel like I am the teenager that has to be in by 10 p.m. when all her friends get to stay out until midnight. I was doing some work with a photographer who gets up at 11 a.m. and starts about two in the afternoon. His creative day begins about the same time mine ends.

My life constantly feels like coitus interruptus. There is little sense of completion. I am always having to scurry off, to walk out in the middle of things. We were doing some photographs in a lovely garden for the fashion show. There was great creative energy between all of us. We took a break and had a picnic with champagne and strawberries. It was lovely. Then I realized, "My God, it's 2:00! I have carpool." I had to leave right in the middle of everything.

I keep thinking that next week I will have more time, but next week comes and there is an endless new list of tasks to be juggled. I keep chasing my own tail. I have many more examples, but I have to go right now. I haven't got time to tell them all.

Margaret Grundstein

SAXOPHONIST

Laura Newman, 28, is a professional saxophone player who has recorded, produced and written music for numerous music groups.

The fact that the instrumental jazz field has been, and is, one of the most completely male-dominated art forms was an issue I never thought to consider until I was already well into my career. As I look back at what disadvantages being female might have posed, I also equally acknowledge the advantages. My overriding drive has so strongly been to play well and grow, there just hasn't been much room to heavily weigh anything else. I think if I had approached my playing fearful of prejudices that I might have encountered, I probably would have found myself in a more discriminated position, for I believe we all find what we are looking for.

There have traditionally been many female vocalists, and a few keyboardists, but certainly not many before me on my instrument, the saxophone. There also aren't many female musicians out in the clubs. I live in Denver, which has one of the best club scenes nationally, and play five to seven nights a week. Certainly, I run into chauvinism and ignorance, but have found that if my sense of humor and sense of the absurd are intact, dealing with it is no problem. I've also observed that even though I might have different types of ignorance to deal with being female, I don't have any higher level of hassle to deal with than the men do.

Currently, I am playing a lot, recording, teaching and have started with a partner the New Cord School of Music. The school is directed toward the adult player, who has just begun to learn to play, or hasn't played since high school or college, or anyone who, because of a busy career, doesn't have other outlets to study and play music. The music is mostly jazz and the courses are mostly playing ensembles. The school has taken off extremely fast which is gratifying because I believe so strongly in adult education and diversification of learning.

My heart is in playing music, which I hope to do on more of a national level, and recording which I would also like to do more of. I'm starting to write and am intensifying piano studies. I am grateful to all those women of courage who struggled not only in the internal wars of creative art, but also with the vast external oppression. I am grateful to have the freedoms of activity, growth and creativity.

Margaret Randall

DEPUTY SHERIFF

Cecilia Kienast, 50, has been a Deputy Sheriff for the past 26 years and is presently a Detective in a Homicide Bureau.

For 26 years I have worked as a Deputy Sheriff in the largest Sheriff's Department in the world in one of the largest counties in the country. The journey took me through the women's jail, Narcotics Bureau as an undercover agent-investigator, and Juvenile and Detective Bureaus, culminating in a lengthy assignment in the Homicide Bureau.

In 1960, I was 24-years-old, very sensitive, gentle, quiet and the mother of two beautiful children. Little did I know the tremendous challenge I had undertaken in this commitment to a nontraditional career for women in law enforcement. This career was to include a wide spectrum of experiences, attitudes and emotions which would tap and develop an inner resource which I chose to consider spiritual. From this experience came much of my evolvement into a mature and confident woman who is a competent and dedicated Detective-Sergeant. I have remained sensitive, but I am no longer quiet and have developed a sense of humor about most of the negative experiences of life.

The "work" was always challenging and interesting, seldom boring. The difficult part was not in the problem-solving nature of our work as much as the stress involved with the grief suffered by humanity. The women in law enforcement of my era were caught in the midst of great social change as the job moved from nontraditional for women to "almost" traditional. We were exposed to many different attitudes from the men with whom we worked. These attitudes varied from open minded, all encompassing acceptance to utter contempt. We were also exposed to many practices that were biased against women at one end of the spectrum and "protective" of women at the other end. The exposure of these attitudes has developed within me a strong sense of being "centered" which is based in self-knowledge and self-respect as opposed to an "other directed" need for approval. I thank the men in law enforcement who presented the challenge and the painful experiences which led me to this place.

Each job experience is altered by an individual's perception and I believe it is this individuality which takes a "work situation" and molds it into a personal contribution to society. Law enforcement is one of those careers which demands from us a strong personal commitment to seeking truth and to helping others, therefore, such a career is indeed noble. The journey has been challenging, interesting, heartbreaking and oftentimes, devastating. I marvel at the growth of a young woman and mother who began her law enforcement career as a very sensitive and quiet soul and has evolved into a mature and confident woman — a woman who can tenaciously pursue and arrest a violent offender, understanding the circumstances which may have led him to his deeds, but seeing the greater need to protect the general welfare of society.

It has been especially rewarding to have pursued this journey and remained sensitive to the sorrow of victims, the pain of parents whose children are troubled, hurt or missing, and to be able to share in the joy, pain and sorrow of all the people we are in contact with. This has, in fact, been "amazing grace" to have been so fortunate as to be a "working woman" in a career thought to be a man's world and to have come full circle in that career knowing that I have brought to law enforcement the many "womanly gifts" which I have to share with humanity.

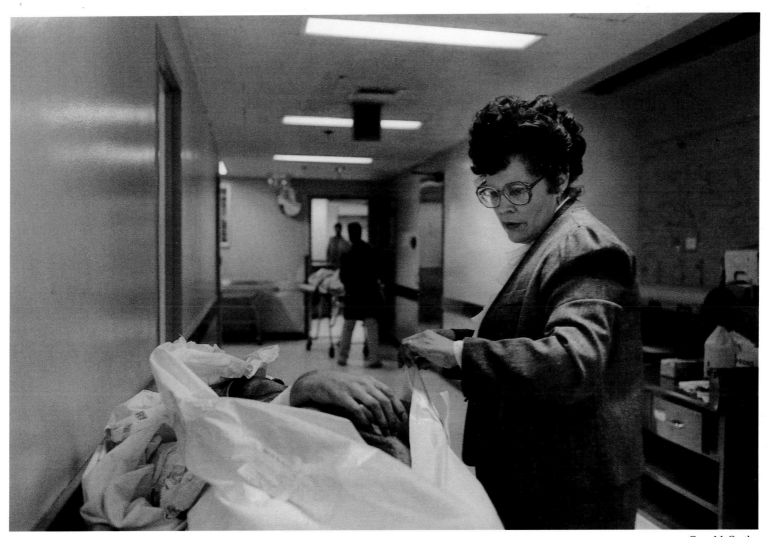

Gary McCarthy

VICE-PRINCIPAL

Evelyn Irizarry, 44, is Vice Principal of an inner-city school in Hartford, Connecticut, and has been in the education field for 20 years.

After graduating from Washington Irving High School in New York City back in 1960, I decided I wanted to be an accountant since mathematics was my "forte." At the time, I did not have the money to go to college so I got a job as a secretary at the Park Royal Hotel with the idea of saving enough money for at least the first semester. But in the meantime, my parents decided to move back to Puerto Rico, and I had no choice but to go with them since they would not allow me to remain on my own. I come from a family of four sisters and four brothers, and we all went back to Puerto Rico.

I attended Catholic University of Puerto Rico in my hometown of Ponce. I had saved enough money for that first semester and indicated on my application that I wanted to major in accounting. I also applied for financial aid which was approved for my sophomore year. I had an uncle, an elementary school teacher, who offered me the money on one condition: Major in education and become a teacher. Reluctantly, I agreed.

I graduated and taught English in Ponce for two years, but the salary was only $250 a month. I was offered a job with Pan Am World Airways, which would be exciting and double the salary. For a year-and-a-half I worked in San Juan, but there was something missing. I really wasn't feeling good about my job. I didn't feel that what I was doing would eventually make a difference in anyone's life. I quit my job and went back to teaching while attending college on a part-time basis, taking graduate courses. I slept better after that, although most of the time I was exhausted.

I have been in the educational field since then and have never regretted being what I am. Eight years ago I was recruited from Puerto Rico because the Hartford school system needed Hispanic administrators. It's an inner-city middle school with approximately 60% Hispanic, 37% black, and 3% white. My job requires firmness, but also flexibility. I must be strict with my students, but also nurturing and caring. I believe in "tough love"; I always make sure my students leave my office knowing I disapprove of the *action*, not the *person.* The kids are beautiful; emotional, honest, sensitive and appreciative.

At times I say to myself, "My God, I can make a difference between good and bad in that child's life. I have something to do with that little person's total formation as a human being. That's power." Kids need structure, but they need an equal dosage of nurturing and love. We all have strengths and weaknesses; I build on the strengths or successes and not the other way around.

Breaking into the teaching field was easy; becoming a school principal was not. Discrimination? Sure! It's always been there and it will always be there. We all discriminate. Some more than others. We discriminate when we choose our friends; when we judge others without having all the facts. I have felt discrimination twice in my life. I applied for a principalship and didn't get the position because I am an Hispanic. You see, the school already had an Hispanic administrator and already had met their quota. The second time around, I didn't get the position because I'm a woman. The general feeling was that the position required the "physical strength" and "power" of a man. Some people believe that a male principal inspires more respect. Naturally, I was not told that these were the reasons, but I can certainly read in between the lines. I must say, however, that these incidents are in my past and I now do not feel discriminated against to that degree.

There have been many rewards during my career. Not so much plaques, recognitions, etcetera, but smiling faces. Kids who have been my students, years later come back with a college degree, a family of their own, a good job. That smile and a "Thank you" is all the reward I need.

WORKING TOWARD OUR GOAL

Gale Zucker

DRY CLEANERS WORKER

Therese Martin Cain, 20, works part-time at a dry cleaners as a trainee on the Community Independent Training for Youth Program. Born a Down's syndrome child, and the youngest of seven children, she has been raised with much the same experiences as her five older sisters and older brother, including family vacations, a trip to Europe and skiing in winter. She was graduated from high school as a Special Education student in June, 1986. Therese dictated the following about her work to her mother.

I work at the cleaners and live with my family. Working in the back of a cleaners is like working in a jungle. I hang clothes by tags, different color tags. Blue is Monday. Red's for Tuesday. Pink's for Wednesday. Orange is for Thursday. Yellow's for Friday. White's for Saturday. I like best to do paper hangers. It's the easiest. I just put the hangers through the paper. I am pretty fast. Sometimes you see spots, then I get Mike (supervisor) to work on the spots.

I like the people where I work. I do like Mike, but there's one thing about him — he's like a good friend. He understands how I feel. Others make nice comments about me like "Terry's great." They know I'm a good worker and I know they like the way I do my work.

Some things I don't like are getting confused when things don't go just right, and when I don't know where to put things when I don't understand. I don't like problems, but I don't seem to be having any now. Sometimes I get tense with Mike when he corrects me.

I'm glad I have the job. It makes me feel good and I like the way people treat me. My boss, Shorty, makes jokes: "Here's your paycheck; go out and get drunk." That was his joke. The ladies who work at the desk up in front are sometimes funny and they are very nice. I think they like to reach out to me, and I like the way they treat me. I think my job is great, though sometimes I get the ups and downs — mad, sad or hurt. If I do, I have to solve the problem.

Gary McCarthy

WRITER

Octavia E. Butler, 39, is a science fiction (sf) writer.

For five years during my childhood, I lived in an apartment building that had once been a small mansion. Pasadena was full of big, old houses gone to seed in those days. I had a bedroom that had once been half-a-pantry. The pantry had been cut in half to give the apartment next door a bathroom. What I had left wasn't much bigger than a walk-in closet. It had a concrete floor and only one window, small and up near the ceiling. All I could see through that window were walnut tree branches and sky. In that room, seated on my bed, surrounded by my clothing and my first books, I did my earliest writing, reveling in horse stories, experimenting with romances, and finally settling in to science fiction.

I also did a lot of hiding in that room. As long as I kept out of sight, nobody expected anything of me. The older people in my family thought I was a nice, quiet kid to spend so much time in my room, out of trouble. But I knew I was hiding. I was tiresomely shy, taller than other kids my age, and thus expected to be more mature than I was. I was clumsy — probably because I was growing so fast. And I was afraid of almost everything and able to make a mess of almost anything.

At some point not long after my pantry room, the house, and the walnut tree had been cleared away to make room for a factory, I began clearing away some of my fears. I began to write consciously, deliberately about people who were afraid and who functioned in spite of their fear. People who failed sometimes and were not destroyed. No one in my earliest writings failed at anything. Their successes were as certain as my failures. But I gave my new characters my own weaknesses and tried to use those weaknesses to bring out their humanity. In my struggles to bring out their humanity, I began to come to terms with my own.

Even now, I give my characters some of my weaknesses and let them struggle toward the strengths I want to create in myself. Constructing my characters still helps me construct myself. And because I write, I'm likely to do things I might be more comfortable not doing. I deliberately allow my writer's need for experience and information to push me into new situations whether they scare me or not.

I grew up surrounded by people to whom survival itself was enough of a problem. They didn't go looking for new experiences or challenges. To them, challenge was concrete. No food, no money, no job . . . Because they overcame their challenges, I had the chance to be challenged by other things.

They, on the other hand, had no chance to understand why I didn't think as they did. To them, writing was, at best, a strange hobby. It kept me out of trouble. At worst, it was a waste of time and parent to my foolish delusion that I could actually earn a living by telling stories.

These people raised me. They shaped much of my world while I was growing up. I was in college before I met other kinds of people — people who learned a language, acquired a skill, created a work of art just because they wanted to. I was in college before I had even one friend who didn't either wonder why I wrote or consider my writing useless unless it made me rich. And at that time, of course, everyone knew science fiction would never make anyone rich.

As a black, a woman, the only child of a shoeshine man and a maid, I am a pretty unlikely science fiction writer. I'm probably the only black woman writing sf for a living — which caused me a problem or two when, at 13, I began submitting stories for publication.

Most of the adult sf I had read then had as its main character a white man who was about 30 and who drank and smoked too much. So I wrote about 30-year-old white men who drank and smoked too much.

But for myself, I had already begun writing the stories that later developed into my Patternist series novels — *Wild Seed, Mind of My Mind, Clay's Ark, Survivor,* and *Patternmaster.* Those were my stories.

Years later, as I helped gather sf stories by and/or about black people for an anthology, I saw what might be called a white adult version of this experience. Most of the stories submitted were about blacks, but written by whites. That turned out to mean most of the stories were about racism. There was an automatic assumption that in stories about black people, racism would be the most important issue, sometimes the only issue.

In 1979 I sat on a panel at a science fiction convention next to the editor of a magazine about science fiction — a magazine that no longer exists, by the way. This editor insisted that the presence of black people in a story changed the character of the story. He suggested that writers who wished to make some racial point in their stories should use extraterrestrials instead.

At the time I decided he was telling more about himself than about science fiction. Later, though, as I worked on the anthology and read all those stories by people who thought writing about blacks meant writing about racism, I thought of him and wondered whether he had been guided by the same mistaken notion. And I was reminded again that I couldn't expect anyone else to tell my stories — or even to understand that I have more than one story to be told.

Patti Perret

CATTLE RANCHERS

Gretchen Sammis, 60, owns The Chase Ranch which has been in her family for four generations. Sammis sleeps in the bed where she was born, and where she ventures to say, "I expect I'll die." Her great grandparents acquired the initial 1,000-acre spread with an exchange of wild horses they had captured, and built an adobe house in 1872, which Sammis lives in today, still using wood stoves to heat each room. Along with her ranch manager, Ruby Gobble, and a

ranch hand, Sammis runs about 250 head of cattle on an 11,000-acre spread situated on the rocky slopes and sprawling high plains at the foot of the Sangre de Cristo Mountains in New Mexico. Sammis was selected to the Cowgirl Hall of Fame, in part because of her conservation work. She also chairs the Northeastern New Mexico Cattle Growers Association. Sammis was a teacher before turning to cattle ranching full-time. She does not talk of retiring or selling the ranch: "It will always be here."

I believe that very early in life an individual sets priorities that he or she is hardly aware of. Deep down, I always knew I would some day be running the ranch and taking care of it. I had the opportunity to, and did, acquire an excellent education. In 1972 I had a good teaching job which I thoroughly enjoyed and I loved every one of my kids. But when the opportunity arose to just ranch I took early retirement and here I am.

Sometimes when it is 20 degrees below, snow on the ground, and calves coming, I know I had rocks in my head to give up teaching. Or when the hay is ready to bale and it rains two inches, I wish I was somewhere else. But not for long. It is a challenging and rewarding life. One just rolls with the punches and hopes to go on forever.

Ranch Manager, Ruby Gobble, 55, grew up on a ranch in Arizona. She learned to work with a rope early in life, and by the time she was 12, broke her first horse, trained him to do tricks, and eventually performed in rodeos. By the time Gobble was 19, she roped calves professionally, and was runner-up for the title of the World's Champion Calf Roper. In 1951 and in 1953 Gobble won the World Champion Team Tying title, and in 1952, the World Champion Ribbon Roping. She first became associated with The Chase Ranch as a ranch manager in 1963. Gobble can shoe a horse, cut a calf, artificially inseminate cattle, handle a bulldozer or cook dinner for company. In 1982, Gobble was inducted into the National Cowgirl Hall of Fame which recognizes women's roles in the settling of the West and the preservation of Western heritage.

I guess I have been pretty lucky. I've done just about everything I've wanted to do. First rodeoing, working with horses, and now ranching. Ranch work is not all riding and working cows. There are fences to mend, hay to cut, machinery to repair and many other things. I have to maintain the ditches, roads and dams with the backhoe and the "dozer." I do all the welding to repair the equipment and build gates and panels when they are needed.

I enjoy working cattle, helping a cow give birth to a calf is very rewarding, but not at 2 a.m. and in zero degree weather! I love the peacefulness of the country, but I also enjoy the people.

Gretchen Sammis

Ruby Gobble

Photos: Barbara Van Cleve

PSYCHIATRIC CHAPLAIN

Barbara Ann Shore, 34, is an ordained Presbyterian minister and psychologist, working as a psychiatric chaplain.

Working as a psychiatric chaplain with mentally ill patients is undeniably both discouraging and stimulating. Political, legal, cultural, institutional, and familial intricacies often seem to thwart effective interventions. Yet, I am convinced that even one person can make a difference in the midst of all these complications and obstacles. One person, trying to figure out what it will take to create or instigate change. Trying to help in what at times appears to be a hopeless situation . . . trying to stop what often seems to be an endless destructive cycle. I am part of an acute treatment team, consisting of a physician, nurse, social worker, psychological examiner, and chaplain.

Raised in a nonprofessional and nonreligious family, perhaps I am not the most likely person to have become an ordained minister and psychologist. I am the only member of a family that did not encourage higher education, to have attended college and graduate school. My parents' views were traditional; women were above all expected to marry. When I entered graduate school, I had no idea as to the amount of prejudice and discrimination I would encounter. Despite the fact that I entered the second largest seminary in the United States, there were no female faculty teaching required courses. A number of the male faculty were quite vocal about their assumptions that the few women in the seminary were there only because they were "man-hunting" or because sexual favors had "earned" them a spot. The prejudice and discrimination within the church has been rampant, and for the most part unchanging, throughout the past ten years. What has changed is that the individuals in power are simply less likely to vocalize their feelings quite as freely. This, regretfully, only makes sexism more difficult to manage and therefore our problems continue. Although women have been able to be ordained in the Presbyterian Church for over 50 years, there is a shamefully small percentage of women ordained. I currently reside in a presbytery that still has never ordained a woman.

Understandably, my initial experiences in the ministry were marked by the fact that above all I was female — for better or for worse. On the one hand it meant continued discrimination, even to the point of job loss when trying to confront sexual harrassment, and on the other

hand, it meant opportunity. Women literally flocked to me for pastoral counseling. Perhaps this should not have surprised me given that one out of every four women is thought to have been physically or sexually abused or raped during their lifetime. These statistics are thought to be even higher within religiously oriented families. Further recent research suggests that between 70 and 80 percent of all persons seeking counseling go to a minister, rabbi, or other religious professional, rather than to a psychologist, psychiatrist, or other licensed mental health professional. This would not be a problem except that the majority of religious professionals have no, or at best minimal, psychological training.

So how did I get to be where I am today? It took the support and kindness of friends, even when they didn't agree with my individual decisions. It took the wisdom of others when I came and told them that I was not so slowly going insane. It took the generosity of persons when I didn't have two nickels to rub together. It took my anger over the world's injustices. It took my fears over meaninglessness. It took determination which some might label as a form of stupidity in my case. It took serendipity, often literally in the form of miracles. It took a sense of mystery. And above all, it took a fundamental belief in the worth of all persons. What were the costs? In the most concrete sense, they were far more than I fear I will ever be able to compensate for. Despite working the entire time I have been in school, I owe thousands of dollars in school loans. I do not own a house, a couch, or even a bed. I drive a 20-year-old car that is broken nearly as often as it runs. More importantly however, were the personal costs. I have never married, and I fear that I may lose the opportunity ever to experience pregnancy and birth. I have been separated from my friends and family for years, although I have had the delightful privilege of making many new friends.

Limited acceptance has come all too slowly and the barriers are encountered daily. Despite ten years in the ministry, I have only had the opportunity of hearing one other woman preach. But the networking grows slowly, as does the opportunity to encourage and support others and to develop uniquely as a female minister. We have distinctive gifts to offer as women, ones that I cannot help but believe will forever change and enhance ministry as we know it today.

Callie Shell

COOK

Olivia Williams, 54, has worked as a cook for the past 20 years.

First of all, I am a divorcee. Being divorced for 24 years, and the mother of five children, I put all five through high school and three through college. I have three sons and two daughters, their ages are 36, 33, 30, 28 and 24. All five live in New York and they all have good jobs. I did not get help from their father at all. When my children were small, I worked ten hours a day to take care of them. When I was coming up, I was told, "If you want anything out of life, you have to work for it." So, that's just what I did.

For 18 years I was a head cook and I worked seven days a week, nine hours a day. And I loved my work. I still love my work. Now, I work at a restaurant and I am over the kitchen, and I do all the prep cooking. I guess you can say I like my job because my boss is nice. He doesn't look over my shoulder while I work. I go to work every morning at 4:30 a.m., six days a week, but on Sunday I go to work at 3:30 a.m. and work until 2 p.m. I guess I would not mind working seven days a week if it was not so hot in the kitchen. When I cook, I have to be in control of the kitchen. I guess that's why I like my job.

I guess you can say I get my will power from God. Every day I ask Him to help me to make it through the day because not all days are good days on the job. Some days I don't feel good, but I go to work anyway. Sometimes I have to go back home, that's why I say God first, then my work.

Laura Elliott

OUTDOOR EQUIPMENT TECHNICIAN

Janice L. Tikfesi, 31, owns her own business, Wilderness Workshop, specializing in fabrication and repair of outdoor equipment for backpackers and mountaineers.

Originally, I started in this business with a partner. I didn't know a lot about sewing or business, but had an interest in backpacking, rock climbing, and outdoor activities in general. Add some money to invest, then throw in a strong sense of dissatisfaction with most (no, *all*) of my previous work situations: *Zap!* One new enterprenuer. Well, the partner ripped me off and left town. Having enjoyed a taste of being self-employed, I decided to somehow keep the business going.

After cleaning up the financial mess and getting the business back to some semblance of order, the next most difficult thing was admitting to myself that it was okay to be a seamstress — that is, to have a "traditional female job." At first, the thought of being saddled with an occupational stereotype rankled me. For example; "Women who sew for a living do so because that's all they know," or, "Seamstresses are willing to work for whatever they can get," etcetera. But as I gained confidence in my ability, as the job of working with my hands and for myself grew, that feeling diminished. All it takes is one customer to come in and say, "I've heard you're the best, that there's nothing you can't do," and a million doubts are blown to hell.

Since becoming self-employed, I've worked harder than ever before. Somehow I don't mind that, knowing it's my show now. No more crap like having some boss say, "Well, you've got to increase your productivity (but don't expect anything more for it,)" or, "Do you have any ideas about how this can be done better? (If so, you'll never get the credit anyway.)" I find that having the ultimate responsibility for a job, from ordering the supplies to writing out the final bill, is a power-ful thrill. Also, there is the very real satisfaction of knowing that a lot of my work goes all around the world. I've done jobs for people who've gone to the Himalayas, the Andes, the Alps — everywhere. It's as though I am there, participating in the expeditions, as though some small part of myself is helping get those folks up there, perhaps with greater comfort and safety.

As a woman owning and operating a small business, I've found that one of the greatest challenges is being taken seriously. Perhaps that has more to do with the size of the business rather than my sex. I still get a lot of people through here who say things like, "Gee, do you actually make enough to support yourself doing this?" or, "Wow, what a neat hobby! What do you do for a living?" Even after four years, stuff like that still has the power to irritate me.

In closing, the bottom line is this: I'm lucky. I'm working for myself in a field related to my interests; I am very good at what I do, and bring home decent money. I guess this is success.

Philip Lebow

SECRETARY

Barbara Howard Black, 28, has been a secretary for the past ten tears. Presently, she works for the Bureau of Labor Statistics.

I have worked for ten years in the government, even working before I finished high school. Office work is a pleasure. Experience has ripened me for about any situation. I can work steadily for hours before realizing that I am hurting my back and eyes by the position and lighting of the work station.

I take pleasure in being able to make a readable object out of a rough draft pasted together. Deciphering work that's hard to read is difficult, and then people want it back right away. I've got to do perfect work, do it on time, and be happy — all at the same time. Usually what happens is on a Friday, they'll give me a big mess and say, "It's due today." Then they leave. So, I have burning eyes and a headache, but it's got to be perfect. Then on Monday, it'll be all ready, and they'll change it all around and say, "Get this ready by 10 o'clock." And then I'm told, "You really do good work." And I'm leaning forward ready to hear some more, lap in the praise, and that's it. That's all.

I didn't get much training on the office machines, mostly it's trial and error. Sometimes you wipe out the whole thing. But I like teaching others. It's good to be able to teach and see the results — how good the person is that you taught. For the first five years, all the people I taught went on to other jobs — they were too good. My supervisor told me, "You're too good." I feel even better that I have learned to master a few office machines in the process. I feel like an expert when it comes to some VDTs, but in this day and age, you have to continually educate yourself to keep abreast of growing office automation and changes .

My kids are what's behind my working. If I don't care for them, who will? I have two children, William age six, and Sharee age two. Public assistance and food stamps is just surviving. If I didn't have the children, sometimes I think I wouldn't be working . . . just be a bag lady or street person. I've been legally separated three years now. My husband sometimes wants to get back together, but I won't do that to myself or the kids.

Through it all, my neck still cramps when I sit still and type too long. But I love typing.

Martha Tabor

TELEVISION NEWS ANCHOR

Bree Walker, 33, is co-anchor of a television nightly news program.

My work is not just a job to me, not even "just" a career. It's a lifestyle. I couldn't do my work well without spending a lot of spare time listening to and watching news, and constantly reading everything from fiction to newsmagazines; I'm functioning well when I'm soaking up information. The never-ending deadlines that are just part of this business add a lot of stress to a working environment already filled with sensory overload. The elements that make this kind of work exciting are the same elements that often make an ordinary day seem like wading uphill, through white water rapids; exhilarating but anxiety producing.

Being a woman in a predominantly male decision-making industry is not a unique situation. There are almost as many female television newscasters as male, but the general managers and news directors are almost always male in this business. Until the status quo is undone, we won't know the effect female decision making will have on the content and style of newscasts. I'm real adamant about equal pay for equal work. That's an important issue of the 1980's that we're going to struggle with, and I don't think this is going to be a particularly easy one with the Reagan Administration so far behind the times as far as women are concerned. Female anchors just don't make as much as our male counterparts. That bothers me.

I was born with ectrodactylism, a severe bone malformation of the hands and feet, commonly called the "lobster claw syndrome." Most people with this syndrome have fingers that are basically, knuckles and fingers fused together in odd shapes; it's the same way with the feet. There's no question that this deformity has affected me throughout my life, and may have been the greatest shaping force in my life. From an early age it taught me not to sweat the small stuff, to just kind of toughen up. My parents allowed me absolutely no time for pity. They just said it won't be part of your life in the home environment and there will be no special privileges. I thought it was a good idea . . . it's what helped me become independent and overcome the feeling of frustration over the little stuff I can't do. It can take me a half hour to button a blouse with small buttons or ten minutes to put on my watch because they don't make watches with the kind of clasps I can do. I cannot remove coins from pay telephones or get coins out of machines because my fingers are too wide and wavey. A lot of tactile skills are impossible for me, but it still doesn't keep me from trying. If I need someone to help me, then I ask. I no longer have my false pride.

When I started working in television, I had to overcome a unique paranoia, *phantom sensitivity*; my concern that viewers might be put off or distracted by my deformity. I worried about it for years before I had the courage and encouragement to make the crossover from radio, where I could hide behind the microphone, to television where every self-conscious gesture would be obvious. But everything was okay; I guess the viewers were as ready to see it as I was to show it. When I was growing up my mom and dad would say, "Everybody has a disability of some kind. You're lucky because yours shows." So people see it, they get over it, and they go onto other things. But for the people whose disability doesn't show, sometimes they're working with a greater handicap.

A dilemma for me as a working woman is how to balance it all. The older I get, the more I would like to have a family. I realize that I've got to do it soon if I'm going to, and I'm in a quandary as to how to balance it all in my life. How not to cheat my children while still getting ahead in the career. It is a dilemma men are not asked to wrestle with and that makes me angry. We are living in a country that couldn't be better off in many ways, and yet our day-care situation is appalling. We're facing a crisis. Every woman I know is in the same boat, trying to get ahead in her work and trying to make room for a family.

Finally, a personal thought or philosophy: I feel extremely lucky to wake up to a job I love to do every day. That's about the best it gets in life. I hope to give back to this world some of what it's given me; a great deal of joy. That's why I like to spend free moments giving volunteer time to charity. My payback is greater than the free time I give up.

Jeff Share

ASSOCIATE PRODUCER

Hali Paul, 32, shares a job with her husband, Howard Brock, as an associate producer for CBS on "The Twilight Zone," and they share responsibilities for their son, Zachary, who is cared for at their work.

As an associate producer, I am responsible for the film from the moment it leaves the lab until you see the show on television. This means coordinating and supervising 14 people who are working on the picture editing, sound work, visual effects, additional photography, stock footage and delivery, both nationally and internationally. When we accepted the position we just assumed Zachary would come with us, as he was still nursing. I think everyone was very surprised when we announced at our first staff meeting that we had a third member of our team! Fortunately, everyone has been very supportive. If I'm in an editing room and Zachary needs to nurse, someone from our staff will call and announce a "Zach Attack." Sharing both job and parenting responsibilities means that Howard and I have to coordinate very carefully. We have to keep each other completely informed about everything regarding both work and Zachary.

Elsa, our childcare worker, cares for Zachary in another building where an office has been converted into a playroom for him. Zachary's room is near the production office. One day I went over to his room, and found that the production coordinator had put up a "Baby Mogul" sign on Zachary's door! People seem to enjoy having him around. I am probably more uneasy about having him at work with me than anyone else. Zachary occasionally sits in at screenings and meetings, but I am careful about when it is appropriate. I worry that having him with me might make me appear unprofessional. Ironically, having Zachary around seems to ease the tension in what can usually be an intense environment. Our office shares a reception area with the producer's office. Frequently, while actors are waiting to read for a part, they will play with Zachary. Once Zachary scuttled after an actor into the producer's office, but he was too young for the part!

One of the guards on the lot checks up on Zachary a few times each day. He looks in on his rounds to make sure that everything is all right. So many people on the lot seem to know Zachary independently of me. When they see us together, they will stop and say, "Oh . . . so you're the mother!" Then they tell me about Zachary's latest activity.

Zachary spends about two hours a day with us while we are working. He plays with the telephone in our office or goes into the next office and finds a member of our staff to play ball with him. Sometimes when Zachary is with me at work, I feel torn. I want to hold him and play with him and give him all my attention. At the same time, I enjoy my work and derive a great sense of satisfaction and pride from it. It is always a challenge to be a working mother, but I am fortunate to have Zachary at work with me. It makes like just that much easier.

Margaret Grundstein

BARTENDER

Jackie Cole, 50, works as a bartender, starting her life anew after the end of her 28-year marriage, and her primary role as homemaker.

I was the oldest in my family, and the youngest of my two brothers was 19 years younger than me, and a year younger than my oldest daughter. My dad did construction work, and my mother stayed at home. It was a very old fashioned Latin family. I got married when I was 16 and my husband was 10 years older than me. We had four kids, including a set of twins, and there were 15 years between the oldest and the youngest of the kids. I stayed at home and took care of the family like my mother had. My husband left me for another woman after 28 years of marriage. We still had three kids at home, and the youngest was 13. I had to support the children by myself and didn't get any help from my husband.

When I was first married, somebody told me, "Don't ever be left with nothing. Always pigeonhole something." I didn't for a lot of years, and then my husband started making good money, so I put some of the money away in a safety deposit box. I thought, "Someday something will come up and we'll have some money." Well, the time came and the money was for me. I didn't do it for that reason, but it just happened to be there at the time that I needed it, so I was able to take care of the kids and myself. It was very hard. For almost two years I didn't go out and look for a job. Finally, one day I said to myself, "This isn't going to get it, you've got to do something with your life."

When I went for an interview at an aerospace company, I told them, "Hey, I've been married all my life, I've never had to work. If you're willing to train me, I'm willing to learn." When I started to work, I was in my 40s, and my job with the aerospace company lasted for about two years before I was laid off. Bartending was sort of "handed to me." A girlfriend was leaving the job and wanted me to take over. I had never spent much time in bars but I like people and get along good with them, so I took the job, and learned as I went. I was shy at first, but it was good for me. It made me talk to people and be more open.

Now, I work at a different bar, and also work part-time in an office in a country club, but I mainly make my living at bartending, and plan to for a long time. I like it. I can be a different person behind the bar. There's a barrier there. I can be more outgoing and friendly, but no one can touch me. I only allow them to go so far, and I never let them lose their respect for me. I always have to draw the line. It was hard after 28 years of marriage, and the rejection of being left, to deal with men again, but tending bar has helped me learn. Relationships are a no no . . . I don't want to get close, but when the time's right, it'll happen. To this day I don't trust, and that's not really good.

I used to have a big house, but I didn't need it anymore, besides I had to sell it to pay the I.R.S. because of my husband's back taxes. But that probably was to my benefit. All things happen for a reason and so far, in a way it's all worked to my advantage. Now, my son and I live in a cabin up a box canyon. It's just 30 miles from downtown Los Angeles, but we've got 40 acres with nothing but a few other cabins and hills around us. We use the fireplace for heat, the oven runs on butane, and I've got room for my horse. I used to ride motorcycles when I was married. Now, besides my horse, I shoot pool for a hobby, and I love to dance.

I basically think of myself as a homebody. I always enjoyed taking care of a man, and I miss it sometimes — but I don't think I could ever give up my independence completely again. I was with one man for 28 years and never allowed to be myself. Now, I know myself and I'm happy with myself. I can tell people what I want, and I do what I want. I like my job. I have good relationships with my children, and I'm very happy taking care of me. I guess I just like me better now than I ever have before.

Mary Ann Wuebker

STATIONARY ENGINEER

Cinthea Fiss, 30, is a Stationary Engineer, and part of a 12-person crew maintaining a 52-story high-rise.

Stationary engineers maintain machinery and operate physical plants. This includes heating ventilation and air conditioning, pumps, electrical systems, domestic water and plumbing, emergency diesel generators, fire and life safety systems, and the automatic controls that run all of these systems. Stationary engineers work in factories, waste-water treatment plants, hospitals, hotels and office buildings. I've been working in a high-rise office building for over four years.

I just recently completed a four-year apprenticeship program sponsored jointly by the employers and the union. The apprenticeship program is an excellent way to learn a trade because one is not expected to know anything at first. All you need is the desire to learn. Besides learning skills from journey level engineers on the job, I also attended evening classes with the other apprentices. We studied air conditioning and refrigeration, machinery, boilers, electricity, welding, blueprint reading, safety, and the history of unions. I learned how to repair and rebuild equipment that previously I never even knew existed.

The building I work in is 52-stories tall, containing two million square feet. The engineers are responsible for maintaining a safe and comfortable environment for about 8,000 workers. There are 12 engineers to cover shifts seven days a week, 24-hours-a-day. Work is always varied, solving new problems, learning new skills, keeping up with technological advancements. One day I might be adjusting thermostats, balancing the airflow in a tenant's space, and the next day I might be programming computerized power demand analyzers to monitor electrical consumption.

Then there are leaking pipes to repair, stopped up drains, electrical shorts, overloaded circuits, preventative maintenance on all the machinery, (fans, pumps, heat exchangers, chillers, generator), chemical treatment, mechanical seals to change, pumps to rebuild, refrigeration units to repair, broken switches, and so on. All the other engineers in this building since it opened in 1970 have been males. I am the only female on the crew. I believe that the sexism I confront on my job is no greater than that which women face everywhere, except that it may be more blatant in a nontraditional, blue collar job. Sometimes, the sexism has been to my advantage. For instance, their expectations of my abilities were so low that it was easy to astonish them with my competence.

Many females that work in my building are secretaries, lawyers, accountants and stockbrokers. By comparison to their expensive, uncomfortable clothes, I am thrilled to be able to wear a uniform, provided with laundry service by the employer, and very comfortable work boots. I get a lot of supportive comments from women in my building, and many questions on how to repair this or that. Some women are interested in getting in the blue collar trades where union contracts guarantee equality and substantial pay and benefits. I usually recommend they start with an apprenticeship program and refer them to organizations which have listings of apprenticeship programs in the area. I certainly hope they go for it!

Raisa Fastman

WELDER

Bessie Lee McHenry, 33, is a mechanic welder at a shipyard.

After graduating from high school in De Ridder, Louisiana, in 1971, I worked at several different jobs in different cities for a couple of years before finding my work as a welder. I started out by joining Job Corps and moving to Albuquerque, New Mexico, to learn how to be a keypunch operator. That didn't work out after a few months, and then I moved to North Carolina with my best girlfriend. I was there for three weeks and found a job working as a "curb girl," taking food outside to the customers in their cars. It was hard trying to make tips, and sometimes, I would go outside in the rain, snow, and cold and still no tips. I worked there for three months and then went back home to Louisiana.

It was hard trying to find a job in my little hometown. My oldest sister was working at the Officers Club on an army base in Louisiana. I applied for a job at a commissary branch and was hired as a cashier in 1972. I worked there for five months, then I took a leave of absence because I was pregnant with my first child. My first husband was in the army, and after we were married, he had to go to Germany. I lived with his mother until he got out and then we moved to Mississippi. He was going to school to become an electrician and we were living on his G.I. Bill. I got a job working at a shrimp factory and came home everyday smelling like fish. My husband didn't like that, so I quit. We were going from one motel to another, until he got a raise, working at a shipyard, and we moved into a small house. That's when our marriage problems began. He would stay out late at night and women were calling all the time to speak to him. I tried to talk to him, but he would beat me and call me all kinds of bad names. I was very depressed.

One day a girlfriend told me about a job making $25 a week. I was desperate for a job, so I took it. The place was a bar that was run down and they gambled in the back. All I did was serve beer and shoot pool all day. After awhile I quit that job too. Then a neighbor told me about the local shipyard needing a tacker, welder and burners. I applied and ended up eventually becoming a Journeyman Welder after working and going to welding and burning school. When I started working, making fair wages, my husband stopped going out

a lot. We decided to buy a home, furniture and a nice car. Everything was going fine until a woman called my house and told me she was pregnant by my husband. He denied it, but the judge told him to pay child support. That's when I decided to end this marriage and move to California.

After moving to Oakland, it took me awhile to find a job welding with only one year's experience. After about four months I was called up for a job with the Boilermakers Blacksmith Union for a job at a small ship repair yard. While I was preparing to take the test, I had several men trying to tell me how to weld. I was nervous being the first woman welder to work in that yard. I passed the test and was hired the next day. After nine months I was laid off, and once again without a job. Then the union called me for another job at a shipyard and I've been there for the past nine years. That was the best thing that could have happened to me.

We get navy ships sometimes which keep most of us working for awhile. To weld on these ships you must be certified in all types of metal, and welding rods in all positions. I have most of my certification papers. Sometimes it's hard working on these ships; we have to pull welding lines and burning lines all over the ship. Sometimes I have problems working with different men in different crafts. Some old men are still prejudice against women working in the shipyard. When I have to work with some of these men, it makes my day a bad one. They ask why I decided to work in the shipyard. I tell them because I needed a job to take care of my kids. Some of them be joking and some are serious. I have been around prejudice all my life, so I can tune that type of stupidity out.

I met my second husband at the shipyard in 1977. We work together sometimes, he is also a certified welder. We get along great at work; he understands about working with all those men. At home, he helps me around the house sometimes. We have three daughters, ages 18, 13, and four and they keep me busy. Sometimes I come home from work and keep right on working. My husband cooks dinner, helps wash and whatever I ask him. I couldn't have a nicer man and hope it stays that way. I'm proud of myself to have chosen this trade and succeed. It has done wonderful things for me and my family.

Nita Winter

POLICE OFFICER

Valerie Lynn Simmons, 26, has been a police officer since 1979. She was rated the best in her police academy class in firearms with a 99.4% average, second place academically, and the top woman in physical training.

The first thing most people ask me when they learn that I am a police officer is, "What made you want to be a police officer?" There are several reasons. First, it was a challenge for me; women weren't supposed to do a "man's job," so I wanted to see if I could do it — I could! Secondly, I felt that I could help others — not change the world — but help. Thirdly, I liked the variety, there's not much time for boredom out here, unless you work the 11 p.m. to 7 a.m. shift on a Sunday.

During my career I've developed a lot of confidence im myself . I've seen things that I hope I never have to see again. I've seen a lot of sad out there like a mother shot down by her husband while she was holding her four-year-old son's hand. How do you explain that to a child? I saw a three-year-old run over by a dump truck; he didn't even look injured, but died later of internal injuries. I've seen several fatalities (car accidents) and thank God, I didn't have to deliver the death messages. There's a lot of pain in this, but I still feel a need to be out there. Sometimes dealing with it is hard, but I've got good friends and close family to talk to about it. The hardest for me is seeing elderly people and children hurt. I think all police officers are that way. I've cried about some of my cases, sometimes when I got off duty. You've got to be able to release it.

My first experience at "proving myself on the street" came after two months with my second partner. We had gone to a "harassing phone calls" complaint in which an irate ex-employee was calling the manager of a hotel and threatening to kill her. The ex-employee was drunk. We apprehended the ex-employee while she was en-route to the hotel and upon finally getting her stopped in the car, my partner ran up to the driver's window and I covered the back. I saw the woman reaching into the console and pulling something out and I drew my weapon and aimed, yelling to my partner to grab her. He did, just in time, because when I got in her car I found a loaded 38-caliber handgun half way out of its gun pouch. She told us she was going to kill the manager, too. After that, I was a lot more readily accepted by my shift/fellow male workers.

Since I was hired in February of 1979, I have worked in Criminal Records, Sex Crimes-Detective Division, Building Security, undercover Metro Division, and my favorite and current assignment, Uniform Patrol. At one point, I went to Metro Division on a temporary assignment, undercover, buying drugs. I guess I was the guinea pig. I'd buy and the guys would come in behind me and make the bust. I was the only female in the division and I don't remember a day I went out there without being scared. I was always afraid that if the deal soured, they wouldn't get there in time to bail me out.

I've been divorced for three years, although the failed marriage had nothing to do with the job. In fact, I still haven't seen a man so supportive of my career as my ex-husband. Most men are threatened by the fact that I'm a police officer. I hear, "You don't look like a police officer." (What's a police officer supposed to look like?) I've been told that I'm "too tough" and some men have even said, "I can't handle a woman who's stronger than me." I don't feel any different from other women, except that I know how to protect myself and others. I still have goals and dreams and needs just like anyone. In fact, I reached one of my goals in February, I bought myself a house! That's where my time and resources are spent now. Doing the work I do, I tend to be cautious with people. I keep a wall up, both on and off duty, because as an officer you never know what will happen.

My outside interests are varied and include karate, cross stitch and writing poetry. But mostly, I love dancing. I used to enter several dance competitions in country & western dance and my partner and I won some. I've been working shift for seven-and-a-half years and I really wonder if I could be content working a 9 to 5 job. I'm proud to work as a police officer and I feel pride everytime I put on my uniform. It's not easy, but I wouldn't trade what I do for anything.

Mark Saltz

MAIL CARRIER

Ahna Fertik, 43, has been a mail carrier for the past 16 years.

I n 1970 I became a mail carrier because I wanted a job with no
mental pressure, I get enough of that after work. I quit smoking,
lost 15 pounds and now enjoy a healthy body at 43 years old. I tend
to be sedentary. They pay me to exercise. This work has been a
physical release and support for me. Most of the time I go home
refreshed. When I don't feel good at work it is an indication of bad
diet rather than a taxing job. I am grateful for the grace that allowed
me, a college grad, to stick with a nonmentally-challenging job. This
ran contrary to my social conditioning. Being a *female* carrier ("mail-
man lady"), however, was always a free twinkle in the eyes of my
surprised addressees. Less so now than a decade ago.

You can tell a lot about people by the mail they receive and the way
their houses are kept. The front of each house is like a cover of a
magazine. Turn a few pages and I'm in the front doorway while the
person is signing for a special letter. I'm being bombarded by information coming from inside the house. Smells, colors, sounds, temperature. Sloppy or neat are textures also. Many people leave the
television on constantly for company. Christmas is my favorite time
of year. I get to feel like Santa Claus everyday, delivering warm
greetings and gifts. There is so much junk mail nowadays that sometimes the act of delivering a personal letter will put me in an altered
state.

There is a house on my route whose mail slot is situated under a
window. A large mirror hangs inside facing the window. Looking
through the window into the mirror, I can see the mail dropping into
the room. Jean Cocteau in his 1949 movie "Orpheus," indicated the
passage of time with a close-up shot of a hand dropping a letter into
a mail box. I think of this every time I look into the window and drop
mail through the slot. I see the letters slipping down the wall, disap-
pearing to the floor below. It is an eerie yet personal moment . . .
something about my death and the interconnectedness of things.

Irene Fertik

PROFESSOR

Rebeca Alice Rangel, 34, is an Assistant Professor/Lecturer specializing in Mexican American Studies and Women's Studies.

I grew up in Fresno, California, with six brothers, a sister, and my mother. When I am asked what made me want to go to school and do the things I've done, it's hard to talk about it because for me part of growing up meant not dwelling on the difficulties, but instead taking those hard times, learning from them, and moving forward.

My mother raised all eight of us by herself. She is my *soul* source of inspiration and strength. At the age of 12, she gave me an incredible amount of responsibility, like paying the gas and phone bill, and getting money orders for the rent. She always seemed to trust my judgement and made me feel like there wasn't anything I could not do. She is a rock of Gibraltar who always finds humor in the most desperate situations, and is highly intuitive to any disturbance going on with me. I find this to be a special kind of communication, especially since I live 160 miles from her.

From the early age of eight years old, I have had a real curiosity of people and the ways in which they interact and treat each other. At about 18, I began noting the ways people treat each other according to their social, economic and often times race, and it became an obsessive interest for me. I went to college for ten years, where sociology, the study of people and race relations, was always a part of my studies.

Now, as a Chicana academic at San Jose State University, my lecturing format and content are unique. I believe students need to make connections between their lives and the rest of the world. Learning that academia is more than obtaining a degree and earning a six-digit income is one illustration. Developing students' awareness of social conditions and the political process around them is another. The focus of my lecturing and research is demonstrating through Mexican and American history, and personal example, role models which exist for Latinas, specifically, and all women in general. This is critical in helping them to create positive social and political change for everyone. Latinas are an energetic, heartful and creative force in society that has yet to be tapped extensively in major decision making roles in our society. Equally crucial to the above is honoring one's tradition while developing feasible alternatives for oneself. This is an integral aspect of this process.

Currently, my research focuses on single-head-of-household Latinas. I am also working on a book for Latinas, specifically, and all women in general, on consciousness raising and empowerment because it is long overdue and necessary. Part of my task is finding funding sources to assist so that I can commit my undivided attention and energy to the book. I have gone through two masters programs and am currently preparing for a doctoral program at U.C. Berkeley. With my book, I want to share my strengths and resources with other women, specifically those in the most desperate of social and economic situations. I hope when women read my book they'll come away knowing they do have choices. Women are incredibly strong, acknowledging that strength is one place to begin.

Douglas Robert Burrows

INTENSIVE CARE NURSE

Lindsay Elizabeth Hamilton, 32, is a registered nurse specializing in intensive care for newborn babies.

Why am I here? Well, I suppose that means, why am I a nurse who takes care of babies? Way back when, I wanted to be an English teacher. But I was a very practical sort, and have never been one to take more than moderate risks — plus the shortage of teaching jobs was worsening. So I looked at the possibilities, and I saw nursing as something I knew I was capable of. And even though I was a budding feminist, I wasn't quite brave enough to go to medical school — it sounded too long, too hard.

So here I am, a nurse. In school I went through quite a lot and I almost changed my mind; but I made it through and emerged into adult critical care. I enjoyed, then as now, taking care of one or two patients at a time, and for several years I handled it quite well emotionally. After awhile though, it all seemed too sad (my father's death occurred during this time), so I quit my job and traveled for a time. All the other job possibilities I looked at then seemed either just as hard, or boring, or I couldn't make as much money. So when my account dwindled, I signed on with a registry to do temporary work in intensive care. At one point, they asked me to work a day in an intensive care nursery; I tried it, and gradually moved into regular intensive care nursing. Once I found my present job, I knew I'd found a job I liked.

Working with babies is very happy most of the time. I see my patients go through lots of crises and emerge fairly healthy. Not many babies die, and when they do, it is sad, especially when it is sudden and unexpected — but this is rare. We've cared for many one-to-two-pound babies who have survived quite nicely. It's amazing to see them grow from tiny red squealers into plump yellers. I also enjoy watching inexperienced parents develop confidence and skill in caring for their little ones.

Sometimes my work is very stressful. When all the babies are crying at once and there aren't enough hands, I can get easily frustrated — I don't like to leave newborns to cry. When my assignment includes an ill infant and another, perhaps a growing preemie, most of my attention goes to the sicker one, and I end up feeling like I ignored the other one. At times, the parent(s) of a baby will react in unpredictable ways, sometimes hostile, or just need lots of attention that I don't have time to give, and this frustrates me too.

In general though, our unit is one where there is emotional support for everyone. We try especially hard to support the parents of the babies because it is extremely difficult for them. It goes against the grain of most new mothers and fathers to be separated from their infants. It is upsetting for them to watch, and wait, and wonder what will happen, and then have to leave the baby with us. There is support amongst the staff for each other, and this is important, for I am a very emotional person, and I need lots of positive input to maintain balance.

Of course, I am working to be paid, as are most people. I do feel fortunate that I enjoy my job. There is a positive emotional climate here. And I absolutely love the babies. They come in all shapes and sizes and colors, like a flower garden. I get a lot of satisfaction in helping them start their lives in good health.

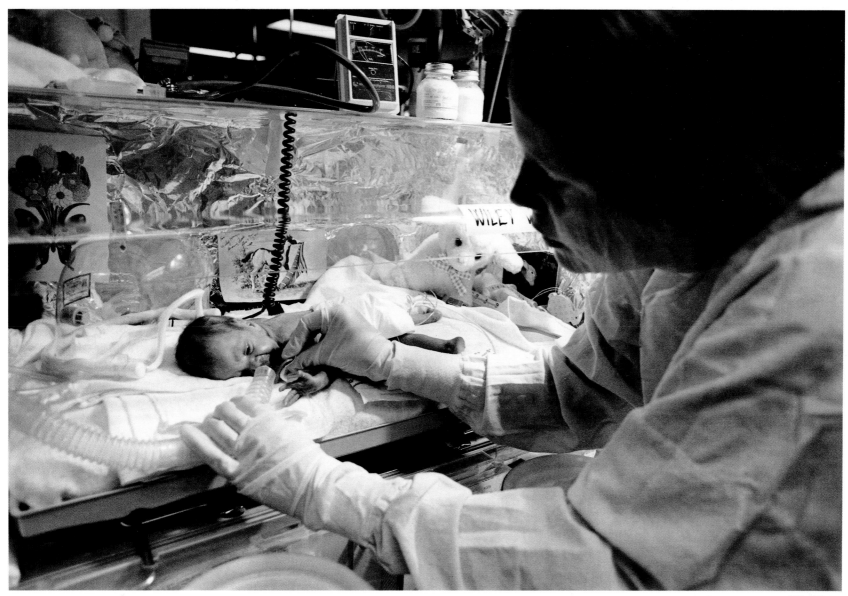

Nita Winter

FARRIER

Ada Gwendolyn Gates, 43, has been a horseshoer for 15 years.

Entering the trade, I never had any fear about doing a "man's job." I just wanted to work on feet because I was fascinated by how a horse moved and thought the blacksmith was the most important person who attended a horse. However, as I started in the business I saw people's faces change and darken when I'd show up to do the job. I'd hear an excuse about why I couldn't do a particular horse. Reoccurring instances that pointed up my "gender" as a competency factor rather than my actual work, instilled an extra anxiety I had never had before in any other job.

My womanness had never been a factor until this job. I started to get paranoid and resentful at times. It made me perplexed and anxious about something so stupid. I'd rather just worry about doing the job right and forget all that extra baggage. That was 15 years ago. Now, I have men clients and peers with whom there is no conflict at all. We have a problem, we solve it together and it's deliciously clean and clear thinking; there's even an extra confidence of liking and wanting to help each other.

I probably go out of my way to help or befriend other women in the horse racing industry. I am a girl . . . I like a "girly-girly" once in awhile and I respect other women who are out there slugging away at it too. One time three of us ganged up on the top vet at the track. We started kidding him about how many wives he paid alimony to and was that why he was always raising his price and working so hard. He joked back for about two minutes and then I watched this pillar of authority blush and run away.

I love the job. It's easy and there's always plenty to learn. I go to clinics and conventions, read and write articles, and love to meet people in my trade who are experts in their divisions. I am never 100 percent confident, however, that I've done exactly the right thing for a horse with a problem. It nags at me, "Did I miss something?" I'm my own worst critic. I *know* when it's *wrong* however, and I jump in and change it. I get mad at myself when I've forgotten something I should have thought of. I don't think I forget it the next time, though.

Presently, in my spare time, I am working in television as a producer and commentator. I feel very comfortable doing the job. I feel no separateness as a woman that I still feel lingers after all these years as a horseshoer.

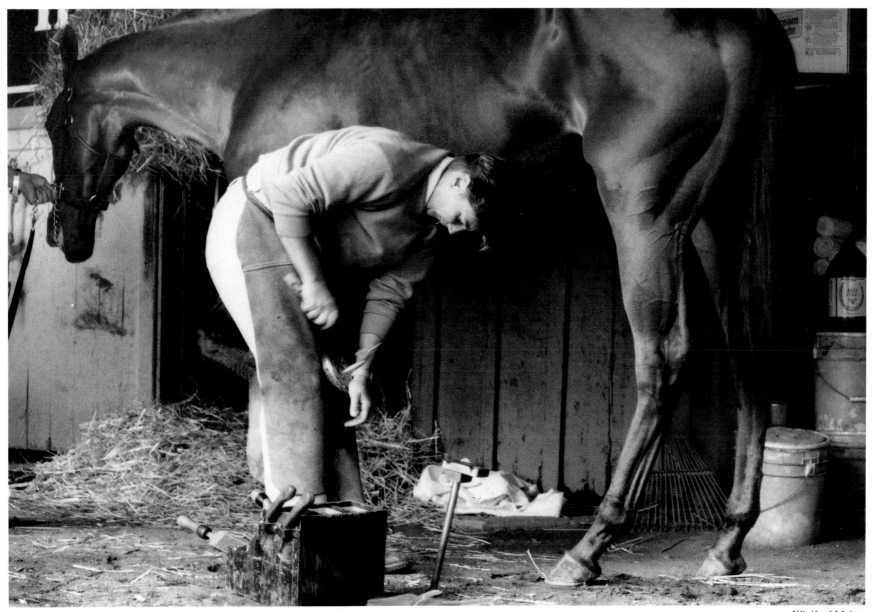

Winifred Meiser

PHYSICIAN

Mai Ting, 41, is a medical doctor based in Santa Fe, New Mexico.

From the time I was a little girl I always knew I was going to be a doctor. There was a sister, before I was born in China, who became very sick with diptheria because during World War II in China there was no immunization program available. My sister, Jen Jen, became terribly ill and could not breathe. My parents took her to the hospital, but the doctor refused to do the tracheotomy until he was paid. It was Saturday night, and my father rushed around the town borrowing money from friends. When he returned to the hospital, my sister was dead, laying in my mother's arms. My parents decided to have another child and that child was me. This has been a great burden to me, and also an inspiration. Now, after many years of being a doctor, I accept the road which fate has set for me. I firmly believe that all people deserve access to medical care regardless of ability to pay. Health is a prerequisite to the pursuit of happiness.

After I finished medical school, internship and residency, I was personally disillusioned with the practice of medicine in this country. This was in the late 60s when so many of us were disillusioned by the American way of life. I chose in the face of war, a quest to find inner peace. That quest took me to a remote rural valley in the mountains of southeast Colorado. I learned to love that beautiful, desolate valley. Facing a minus 40-degree temperature in a raging blizzard was easier for me to deal with than a drunkard's accusation, "Hey, China girl — when I was in Shanghai during the war . . . "

There were other people who were drawn to the valley during those years in search of alternatives. As we built our families and our homes, it became obvious the community needed health care services. People would come to me for help and advice. After a particularly bitter experience trying to help parents find medical care for their sick baby who was bleeding internally, I decided to get my medical license to practice. It wasn't an easy decision. I like my privacy, I like my freedom. I knew my family's life would be disrupted.

People say doctors make a lot of money — remuneration for our time. I haven't found that to be true, especially if you're taking care of poor people, and they can't necessarily pay you well. Most of my patients have tried to pay me something, but there are those who justify in

their minds that the time I spent wasn't really worth it. That it was more important to buy a car, a satellite dish or a six pack of beer. And I guess those are the ones I remember when I'm feeling "burnt out" and "used." But there are also those really special moments when there is a smile, like when a baby is born, that makes it all worth while.

I've moved to Santa Fe to work at the penitentiary of New Mexico. It's a hard core prison as far as prisons go, but I took the job because I just wanted a job. The inmates are locked up so they won't be bothering me whenever they want, and it affords me the time to spend with my children. I'm also working with Women's Health Sources in Santa Fe which was started ten years ago in the wake of the women's movement as a cooperative. It serves the poor people in Santa Fe and as a result of not being able to obtain public grants, it's always on the brink of financial disaster. The center paid their last doctor $12.50 an hour. We're going to try and provide more services with the growing needs of women, but why am I doing it? Perhaps because it challenges me, it gets me excited, because *they* said "it can't be done." Of course, I'm going to have to get another job to help pay the bills.

Where is it all going for me, being a doctor in the United States in 1986? Not to a good place. There's too much paranoia; *malpractice* looms above our heads. Americans are too busy buying things with a 50,000 mile warranty. They want Life translated into a guarantee. And how does a doctor guarantee you a perfect baby, a perfect operation, a perfect cure? I know for years I wanted nothing to do with obtaining malpractice insurance. To me medical care was an agreement between the doctor and the patient — a bond of trust between two people. I thought that if I tried my best and taught the patient to accept responsibility for his or her own health, I could avoid a malpractice suit. If I can't operate on this principle, it just doesn't make sense to me to even practice medicine. Well, I ate my words. I now have malpractice insurance because the hospital in which I work and the board of directors of the clinic think I should have malpractice insurance. Anyway, I let them pay for it.

Martha Tabor

OIL LEASE OPERATOR

Sally Ulman, 29, is an oil lease operator.

To many, a woman working in the oil fields would seem somewhat unusual. To me, it's just another adventure. A woman working in a man's environment is a challenge — the challenge to become just another "hand," a blue collar term for a worker. For a woman to be labeled a "good hand" is another way of stating acceptance.

Acceptance by your male co-workers could be complex. If you try too hard by pushing your physical limits or mechanical knowledge, you face the chance of being labeled a "heman." They may back off and give you the feeling, "If you think you can do it all, then do it," and then step back to watch you fail. To go the other direction and ask for help frequently and show either lack of knowledge or lack of motivation to learn, would then get you a reputation, usually labeled "a typical woman." Although I dislike these stereotypes I've been up against from day one, I've learned to deal with them.

To handle these stereotypes I must first realize who the men are that I work around. Many are very conservative, thinking that a woman's place is in the home. For me to ask these men to approve of my presence would be too much. I simply ask for acceptance. To attain acceptance I limit myself on what I can do physically. Most jobs that involve physical work, if you attempt to do it, and cannot, are easy to get help with. If you show motivation and determination, you will have few problems.

To attack a physical job in the presence of men and not expect them to help should not be confused with being nonfeminine. I do like to have doors opened for me and chairs pulled out, but at work I would rather be "one of the guys." Being one of the guys means acceptance, but it could go overboard. If you blend in too much, you may find yourself surrounded by rude behavior and language. To deal with this, in most cases, I need only mention that my status of "one of the guys" pertains to work, not behavior. If I let myself fall into their behavior patterns, they may lose respect for me as a person. You can only be what you are, not what others expect — prove yourself and be yourself.

Acceptance is also hard to maintain. Just as a star athlete is expected to perform at high levels year in and year out, a woman must also do the same. People tend to want something to blame for failure. With a woman, her sex is simply enough in a male environment. A constant, high level of job performance and motivation ensures ongoing acceptance. All in all, if I show that I can, and want to perform the work, most of the men will accept me. When I was first hired by the oil company, I knew I would have to work hard from the start. Talking to most head operators that work with new people, they would rather have hard working women in their crews because they say the women aren't afraid to work and they tend to do more. The men feel that the company owes them a living. I feel as though I have to earn that living. I owe the company eight hours worth of work. I just bought a house and car, so I assume the same financial obligations the men do. I'm single and live by myself.

Everyday I keep maintaining my motivation and I find myself feeling more and more accepted and comfortable in my work surroundings. Although it may be an uphill battle, I look at it as a challenge, one I'm on head to head.

Pam Benham

DANCE HOSTESS

Layla Maye Lorren, 27, works as a dance hostess, also called a taxi dancer, and attends college as a part-time student.

Upon entering the club, one pays a small cover charge and is then escorted to a table where a host will greet you and help select a girl, if necessary. We girls are seated on any one of the three red plastic couches. The customers can see us through what almost appears to be a two way mirror which separates the actual dance club area from the waiting area. Men choose by whatever is visually appealing to them, it's a very random thing. After a selection is made, the host summons the girl and she then signals the front desk where her time card is punched recording the amount of minutes spent with that customer. The club does not serve liquor. Each girl is given a number, I'm #300. When I'm the chosen one, I'm escorted to the man's table where I introduce myself and we begin chatting, and if he enjoys dancing, we trip the light fantastic.

The club has a pay scale, and they pay you by the week. The more minutes you're with men that week, the more it goes up. For the week, if you don't make a thousand minutes with the customers, then you get minimum wage, $3.35 an hour. If you make above that, then you get ten cents a minute. And if you get 1300 minutes a week, you make 13 cents a minute. I make about $400 a month, and about another $400 in tips, working six hours a night, five nights a week.

I personally enjoy dancing and plan to take some fall classes at my community college. I just finished my first semester studying beginning theater arts and stage crew. School was the reason I took this job; to have my days free and my nights paid. The men I've met at the club range from young college students to mature businessmen. Of course, I've had my share of creeps, ugh! Nasty ones, greasy ones, filthy ones and sleazy ones, yeeach! But, if somebody irritates me, I merely punch them out . . . on the time card that is. I need not waste my time with them. After all, time is money, especially here. Most of the girls I've spoken with at the club are aspiring actresses and/or models like myself. None of us plan to make a career in here.

I was going to quit because I felt like I was getting a bad reputation, sort of like I was a big joke. I was getting tired of the teasing, but now I don't care. Sometimes my friends would all laugh, or they'd say, "Here comes the taxi dancer." I was embarrassed by what I do, talking to those men for money. I guess it is kind of strange, but it's not that strange. I could be doing something worse than that. I tried some other dancing jobs, like bar dancing and bikini dancing, but I didn't like it . . . I didn't like the men. The dancing was all right, but the men were so close to you they could almost touch you and breath on you. The whole atmosphere was scarey, so I quit, even though I like to dance. I went for some other dancing jobs, but most of them want you to take your clothes off and I don't want to do that. It doesn't leave any mystery. I like to do something where I do a show with a costume on.

I've done just about everything under the sun. All kinds of waitress work, secretarial work, odd jobs, you name it, I've done it. When I was about 13 my mom and dad broke up. My mom lost custody of us, and my dad couldn't take care of us, so he put us in different foster homes. When I turned 18, I was with my father's girlfriend, and then I lived with my mom. She took care of me, I guess she felt bad she lost custody of us because she was drinking. She made up to my sister and me by totally supporting us, and she babied us, and pampered us, too much. So, just now I've become independent, but it's been hard for me because I'm not use to it. I live with my sister right now, and my mom still helps me out with rent, but I want to get out on my own. That's why I'm trying to get two jobs so I can get my own place. I haven't built up enough character to really know what kind of person I am on my own two feet.

Ted Soqui

RODEO BRONCO RIDER

Marge Dressel, 32, is a bareback bronco rider who works at a rodeo school as well as bartending part-time.

Born and raised on a farm in Northern Minnesota, I've always been physically strong — threw hay bales, broke and trained horses, and worked in the woods for my dad who had a pulp contract with a paper company. My mother was killed by lightening when I was four years old, and dad raised four girls, ages four through ten. He taught us to be strong emotionally as well as physically; to go after what we wanted and stand up for what we believed in. I played judo for six years while in high school and took the Minnesota State Tournament as a Brown Belt.

In 1967 I started barrel racing with my mare that I raised from a baby, and still have after 21 years. She was my barrel horse for 13 years and is now one of my pick-up horses at the rodeo. We went to many small, amateur rodeos and I was always fascinated by bareback bronc riding. I always thought I'd like to try it. I had mentioned this to my ex-husband, and of course, he would have none of that! Our marriage was a very stormy, abusive and demeaning relationship for me. I was emotionally and physically abused. After nearly ten years, on my 31st birthday, he put me in the hospital and I never went back to him. The counselors and advocates at the Battered Women Shelter brought me back around and helped me rediscover how full and beautiful life can

be and how much strength, character and love I really have in me. They made me discover a whole "new me" — one that was really there all along. I vowed to myself that no one and nothing, no matter how rough things get, will ever bring me down again. I depend on myself and *go for it* in everything I do and in every part of my life. My new philosophy is, "Every day's a holiday and every meal's a feast!"

I was ready for a change and had the opportunity to move to New Mexico. So, I packed up everything I owned, loaded my horses, and headed south. I began training on a mechanical bull at a rodeo school in Peralta, New Mexico, and a week later I got on my first horse. According to the owner, no woman had ever tried bronc riding at his school, but he figured his horses "were equal opportunity buckers — they will buck anybody off." I made the eight-second ride, but not knowing enough to hang on until the pick-up rider got to me, I fell off and busted three ribs. I rode the following seven weeks with my ribs wrapped, although the doctor said I couldn't ride at all. Painful! But I was hooked after the first ride and nothing was going to stop me. I've been riding one or two horses a week ever since.

My friends and coaches at the rodeo school have helped back me all the way. Of course, I've encountered opposition in a couple of different instances. There are those who figure I'm out there to attract attention or see what I can find to sleep with — not true at all! I'm

there to prove nothing to anyone but myself. There've been rumors started about me and two different cowboys have actually left because women are riding at the rodeo school. My pick-up partner, also a gal, and I have met up with scorn, ridicule and resistance to our being the ones out there, responsible for getting the cowboys off safely after their ride. But we've shown them we do a good job, and we work well together as a team. We've had to work hard to gain their respect, but now most of them are behind us all the way.

I had a setback in December 1985 when I had to have an emergency hysterectomy. I nearly died in surgery and had complications afterwards. I was told I couldn't ride bucking horses anymore and it would be at least three months before I could go back to work or ride even my own horses. I was upset at first, then I got myself in hand and looked at things I'd made it through in the past. I decided this was just another test for me and got myself up and walking around the hospital two days after surgery. I began walking and climbing stairs every day and really pushed myself. I went back to bartending six weeks after surgery and began riding my own horses after seven weeks. Nine weeks after surgery I got back on a bucking horse. My own determination and physical strength helped bring me back in better health and physical condition than I'd been in the last four years.

The owner of the rodeo school has taught and supported me so much!

My coaches have worked with me and taught me, step-by-step, to ride like the pros. My goal is to join the Women's Professional Rodeo Association (WPRA) and compete and win. Those that know me have no doubts I'll do just that. There are those who are skeptical because of my age, 32 years old, and my size, 5'1", 105 pounds — put that against 800 to 1000 pounds of twisting, jumping, kicking horse flesh, and they don't think I can handle it, but I've proven more than once that I can. I ride by men's rules, one handed rigging and using my feet to spur the horse from the point of the shoulder up to the withers.

Riding bareback horses has become a main driving force in my life. I want to be the best and I'm working hard. It's an almost undescribable high feeling! It's like being on a stick of dynamite, not knowing which way it's going to explode — twisting, turning, tossing you up and slamming you down. And all that's holding you on is one arm and your spurs in the horse's shoulders. A mass of muscle bursting angrily out of the chute when you nod for the gate. It's the longest, most exciting eight seconds of your life and the roughest when you climb on a tough one! Yes, I've had injuries: Busted ribs, cracked tailbone, kicked in the chin, stitches, and knocked out a couple of times. But never enough to dull my enthusiasm. I make most of my rides, but I've eaten plenty of arena dirt too! It's great! I don't know anyone who has more fun than me!

Photos: Alexandria King

SCHOOL CROSSING GUARD

Marva J. Holliday, 49, has been a school crossing guard for 16 years.

My dream was to become another Billy Holiday, Sarah Vaughn, Ella Fitzgerald. I sing jazz and blues where and whenever I can. I belong to the Senior Choir and Gospel Chorus of my church, and I'm part of a 50-member choir. A great actress was also a dream of mine, and I am a member of the Drama Guild at my church and performed in seven productions. My role as Lena Younger in "A Raisin in the Sun" was my finest hour. Now, the question is, what do you do Marva?

I am a school crossing guard for the city of Philadelphia and I recently received an award for 15 years of service. I am now into my 16th year and I love my job. My wages are less than $10,000 per year, I work four hours a day and ten months a year. There are no wages or work during July and August, so during the summer months I am a home health aide for a nursing service. I service handicapped and senior citizens in their homes, two to four hours a day and this work is very rewarding.

I have not always been a school crossing guard. I also worked as a telephone operator for about 11 years, and a mailroom clerk for about four years, as well as a cab dispatcher, inventory counter, home health aide, clerk typist, and seamstress. Because I was raising three small children during that time and working at night, I had a baby sitting problem and had to resign from the postal service. As you might guess, there is a time period where I was working two jobs. I am qualified to earn $35,000 per year and have been offered a full-time position with the city, starting salary double my present income. Would you believe I turned it down? My friends have said, "You're crazy," but some people have said if you like your job, stay where you are. I *love* my job.

I love the children and teaching them safety habits in the street. Also, the respect from the community and parents as well as the children. I love the freedom of not being confined indoors and being able to walk to and from work, and all the things I can get done between my working hours.

What I don't like about my job are snowballs. I hate, *hate snowballs*. I don't throw them and I don't like them thrown in my direction. I don't like ice; walking on ice with a constant fear of falling. Also, the arthritis in my legs and hips, sometimes it will not bother me all winter, but when the April rain falls, the good ole arthritis will pay me a visit causing great pain and discomfort. I have a list of things people do that bother me when I'm working as a crossing guard: Red light runners; non-turn-signal users; tailgaiters; red light crossers; middle-of-the-street crossers; and cross corners crossers. The last three are teenagers and adults and their actions will cause children to copycat.

My benefits with this job are the best part for part-time workers. We all get uniforms, including watches, shoes, boots, handbags, and gloves, along with a full dental plan, eye glasses, clinic and hospital benefits, legal services, vacation pay, annual leave days, snow days (four per year), funeral days and sick leave plus eight paid holidays. Yes, I love my job!

Linda Griffith

HAIRDRESSER

Jeanne Carol Lack, 35, a hairdresser for the past 15 years, often brings her child to work.

What got me started in the hairdressing business was my interest in art while in high school which I wanted to continue with, but I felt that the art field was too competitive. I'm the kind of person who doesn't care to compete in anyway, so to me, in some way, I'm still in the art field with my career as a hairdresser.

I really enjoy my work and I've been at this shop for 15 years, and a lot of my patrons have been coming ever since I started there. I'm my own boss, choosing the days and hours I work even though I work for someone. My employer doesn't care if I bring the baby with me. In fact, if I'm in the middle of a perm or color, she helps out by feeding him lunch. I'm happy that I have my son Christopher with me at work because he is my only child and I'm at an age where I really enjoy him.

Sometimes, it gets to be a bit much with Christopher into everything. It's hard when he wants to be held and I'm busy. He starts yelling or pulling on my pants leg, and either I break for a minute and get a bottle or I pass him to my patron while I work. I bring a cooler to keep his bottles and food in; a baby carrier for his naps; and a walker to let him run around in. Christopher has a good time at the shop meeting and greeting the patrons, and getting to know the people I work with. Sometimes, I wish I could stay home with him, but I know I'd miss work, so this way I can do both.

My hubby and I have only been married going on three years. I have two teenaged stepchildren that live with us, so I manage a house, job and children. Cooking for all of us has been rough because they were all coming home at different times. It's to the point now where I cook once and make up plates. I usually start dinner in the morning before I leave for work; throw a roast or chicken in the crockpot and when I get home, it's done except for the veggies. Washing clothes was a problem since we don't have a washer and dryer. But now, all I do is bring them to work with me because right next door is a laundromat. I'll go over, put the clothes in the washing machine; go back to work and do a wash and set; run next door and put the clothes in the dryer; run back to work to do a comb out; go back and fold the clothes; put the clothes in the car; and then back to work I go. I usually do it two times a week. My two stepchildren are like most teenagers, you have to keep after them to do anything, and that's hard for me to step in with them already grown and not being there when they were small. It's like being married to three people.

Problems are few for me at work except when someone overbooks me or I get sick or want time off and have to rearrange my appointments. I'm glad to be able to have my son with me at work. I've reached my goal, if I really had one, with working and running a household.

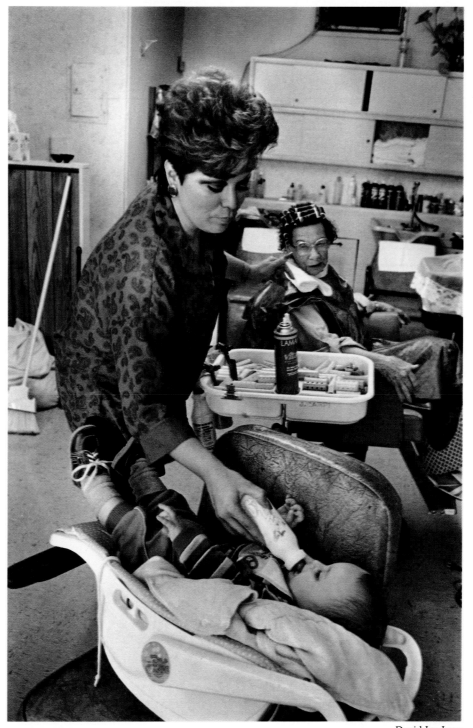

David Jay Lans

WILDLIFE ACTIVIST

Penelope Bishonden, 43, cares for lions and tigers on a private game reserve where she lives, tending to their needs on a 24-hour basis. For the past 12 years she has worked raising, feeding and attending to the health needs of the animals, none of which have been declawed or defanged.

I have had a lifelong preoccupation with cats; from my beloved nanny's tabbies when I was barely two; wanting to comfort the sad old lion in the early Los Angeles zoo; my essays in school on cats; drawing them; bringing home strays; and making my own conclusions as to why the lions didn't eat Daniel. These early aspects led to painting lions to support my young sons and exhibiting in wildlife benefit art shows. If someone had ever asked me what I wanted, my answer would have been "a lion."

Visions do come true, and when my opportunity arrived, 12 years ago, in the form of Tippi Hedren carrying a lion cub, I *knew* I'd never stop until I had "my" lions — as it turns out, I now own several lions, and my lions "have" me! I doubt if anyone has ever been more willingly possessed! I could never give lions as much as they've given me — we are one together, these lions and I. My wish now is to be a worthy translator of lion behavior to those who don't love them, only because they don't know them.

One day perhaps, humans will evolve to the point of allowing wild animals to live the free lives God meant for them. These poor captives of mine have a desperate mission; turning hard human hearts to the task of saving wildlife for the future. We're down to a handful of gorillas, and today, we know they can speak to us and reason. What other *different* but equal companions will we bring to extinction? Whales? Snow leopards? All of them, it seems. Humans cast the first stones, but it's wildlife that is without sin.

Whatever it takes, I will do my part to help wild animals survive. I feel that the three factors that contribute to the demise of wild animals on this planet are human overpopulation, chemical pollution, and exploitation by humans as objects of entertainment and financial gain. If we continue to mishandle the byproducts of our civilization such as radioactive waste and unchecked real estate development, there will be no open land left for human beings, let alone animals. The voice of the lion and whale are inseparable parts of human racial memory . . . when they die, we die. I believe the Great Spirit gave us this earth to cherish and everything we do for wild animals counts. I'm not looking for a heavenly reward, I simply want to do what's right while there's still a chance.

Many people say to me, "I'd love to do what you do" or "I've always wanted to work with wild animals." I think they really mean they want to pet a lion or tiger and have their picture taken with one and walk away. I've never met anyone who really wanted to stick it out. One doesn't "dabble" in lions. I don't know all the answers, and I make many mistakes, but what I've experienced is *real*, and hopefully, I'll meet other people who are willing to face the daily realities of relating to lions and tigers. Children 200 years from now deserve to see wildlife as it's supposed to be — not stuffed in museums or hanging over mantelpieces!

Carol Nye/Steven Middlesworth

ARCHITECT

Elizabeth Ericson, 46, has been an architect for the past 16 years.

Becoming an architect takes a long time. After 20 years in the business, four years of architectural school, and four years of liberal arts education, I am still learning. At 17, I was all set to be a journalist, then I went to the Yucatan and saw the ancient Mayan city, Chichén Itzá. Limestone structures gleamed in the jungle, their geometries crisp and beautiful. Silent cities spoke to me of the human spirit which once inhabited them. I was moved. I decided to study architecture.

I graduated from Columbia School of Architecture in 1966, after an intensive four years of engineering, construction, painting, sculpture, history and principles of design. Living in New York City was an architectural textbook all by itself. After school, I traveled around the world on a fellowship to see the buildings I had only read about. I sketched them. I was elated. But I needed to learn more to become useful to the practice, so I got a job as an office apprentice, and for very little pay. At my first job as a designer-draftsman my lettering was wiggly. I was told that I would be fired unless the letters were straighter and more consistent. Being an architect can be a humbling experience sometimes, especially after all that education.

In 1972, I took the four-day state test, and was licensed to practice architecture under my own name. I had to decide whether or not to stay in the firm I worked in or start my own practice. I decided to start a small office with my architect husband and two employees doing residential buildings. I spent a lot of time in administration, client and employee relations, and not enough time on designing and building. I am now a partner at the Boston firm of Shepley, Bulfinch, Richardson and Abbott. It's the oldest firm in the country with a very young spirit. I am the first woman in the firm in that position, and there are 120 employees.

The specific issues I face as a woman in architecture are the same issues that anyone faces in the profession; namely, *credibility*. What does a woman, especially a woman *designer,* know about technical things? I overcame this doubt by working extensively in the field for awhile supervising construction. My knowledge was firsthand, and better than most architects who stayed behind their desks and drafting tables in the office. To my delight, management issues are shared by all the partners, and I can focus on design and building.

As an architect, I have chosen to humanize and beautify the most technical and sterile of building types, namely hospitals. I see no reason why these very important medical "city states" are any different from those Mayan cities I visited. I like to bring daylight and gardens into medical treatment spaces, and to create vistas and axes to dignify the human spirit, as well as nooks and crannies to offer comfort. I have completed four major hospitals, and they are little by little achieving these goals.

My daily routines include a little bit of everything. For example: I am a member of the Design Council and, with the other design partners, review the design quality of current projects in the office. In the afternoon, I talk with designers working on my projects about their particular problems. I am doing an office building, hospital and auditorium renovation at the moment. I have to talk over budgets with my managing partner; review changes with building owners; make presentations to clients; prepare drawings, and much more. Part of my week is spent traveling. First, to the hospital for the budget review. Then to the college to present design ideas for the auditorium. Finally, I drive to the concrete plant to review the quality of the concrete panels being made for the hospital, now under construction. It's raining and I take my heavy boots. The rosebud granite aggregate is not as smooth as it should be and we discuss whether more vigorous vibration during the pouring of the panel would correct the problem. Each week and each project is different. The work is never boring to me.

What is frustrating about the practice of architecture is that there are so many people involved. Decisions aren't made. They evolve from endless meetings, reviews and budget cuts. It's very hard to emerge with the idea you had in the beginning, intact. The rewards? That one's imagination can become reality. That the imaginative use of space and light can bring dignity and hope into our lives. That one can achieve beauty.

Marjorie Nichols

ZOO KEEPER

Melanie R. Bond, 35, is a zoo keeper specializing in the care of gorillas and orangutans.

One of my first books was *Zippy the Chimp's Birthday Party*; perhaps that shaped my future career! From the time I was very small, I liked animals. I considered veterinary school, but decided I wouldn't like being around animals that were sick or in pain. When I was ready to graduate from college, my dad encouraged me to apply for a keeper job at the National Zoo where he had often taken our family when I was a child. I was one of the first women hired at the National Zoo in 1973, although European zoos had a long tradition of female keepers. Some of my co-workers had a hard time believing that someone with a college diploma would be happy cleaning up after animals, and many of them thought women would be physically and temperamentally unsuited to the work. Some of the gentlemen refused, at first, to allow "us girls" to carry a bale of hay or sack of feed. But after pointing out that we were paid the same wage to do the same work, and that we would ask if we needed help, we soon reached a cordial compromise.

I have worked with small mammals, reptiles and amphibians, and primates, from the tiny, highly-endangered golden lion tamarin to the largest of the great apes, the gorilla, and their Asian cousins, the orangutans. I also cared for Ham, the first chimpanzee in space. I've been working with apes since 1975 and there is no place in the zoo I would rather be. Apes are intelligent, powerful, emotional beings. It never ceases to amaze me that they can be very much like humans one minute, and totally nonhuman the next. But they are never *inhuman* or mock human, and that is one of the most frustrating parts of the job; too many people still see the stereotyped ape — King Kong or Clyde the orangutan caricature of the Clint Eastwood movies. One of my many aims as a keeper is to help educate the public about the *real* apes and their plight in the wild. Most people still come to the zoo primarily to be entertained and it is challenging to find ways of educating them about endangered species and conservation issues.

My primary responsibility is the care of six orangutans and six gorillas who live in the Great Ape House, a job I share with four keepers who divide their time between our building and the Monkey House. The majority of our time is spent cleaning cages, preparing diets and feeding the animals. We also alert the veterinary staff if we suspect one of our charges is sick or injured and assist in examinations, treatment and medication. Finding ways of constructively occupying the time of these curious yet powerful animals is a continuous challenge. They have a short attention span and are easily bored, but are so strong they demolish children's toys in just a few seconds.

After discovering that one of the orangutans liked to play with my fingers, I initiated the use of American Sign Language at the National Zoo and visited several ape-language research projects to study their teaching techniques. Although the gorillas at the National Zoo didn't seem to enjoy the physical manipulation of their hands that was required to make the various signs, the orangutans were very responsive. We don't push the animals to use sign language, and communicate primarily in spoken English which they understand much better than pet dogs or cats. Use of sign language has encouraged an even closer bond between myself and my "red haired friends," allowing me such privileges as a mother bringing her newborn baby to me and placing it in my hands. All of the orangutans respond well to being asked, "Show me your hurt," and allow me to apply topical medications or point out injuries to the veterinary staff.

Orangutans and gorillas live more than 50 years in captivity and one of the greatest things about my job is being able to keep them healthy, happy and safe, and watch them grow and develop from helpless infants to handsome adults. Building a relationship of mutual trust and affection with entire families of these wonderful beings is a feeling that can't be put into words, but can be seen and appreciated by thousands of zoo visitors. The best kind of job satisfaction comes at the end of the day when the last meal is fed, and I can spend five minutes of quiet time with five-year-old orangutan Indah, sitting in my lap, long red arms around my neck, feeling like there is no place else I'd rather be! And having a group of children just outside the glass cage front, eagerly waiting to ask questions and learn the real story from the ape's best friend!

Martha Tabor

MAYOR

Julene Pepion-Kennerly, 45, is the first Native American woman to be elected mayor in the United States. In addition to being Mayor of Browning, Montana, the largest community on the Blackfeet Indian Reservation, she is also Director of Social Services for the Blackfeet.

Someone once told me I had a lot of love to give, go give it. I didn't know what they meant. I guess I'm beginning to see what they mean now. I would describe it more as caring about our fellow human beings. I was asked to write about myself, I don't know what to say, for fear I will sound like I am conceited. But I am proud of who I am, what I stand for and what I've been. I've been to the pits of hell, actually felt the fires of it, and the darkness of despair. I had to go through all that in order to feel and do what I am doing now.

I never knew who I was before that time, I didn't have an identity. I was my father's daughter and from there I was my husband's wife and my two sons' mother. Never was I Julene Pepion-Kennerly, until the last five years when I began to find out who I was and what I stood for. I am a unique Half Breed Indian. I was a wife and a mother and I am at last myself. I can make sound decisions and be responsible for them. I am the sole supporter of myself now, the first time ever I have had to worry about if I am employed or not. I always worked, but I never worried about too much because I knew my husband would always take care of me.

I got married a year after high school to a neat man who gave me a lot of inspiration to life. I had come from a family of nine children, tragedy hit early in my life, as so many Indian families are. I would say 90% of the families on the reservation have suffered the effects. My two sisters died in a car wreck which I witnessed at the age of 14. My two sons died of RH factor early in my marriage. My mother died of cancer and my father of heart failure. My brother is paralyzed from the neck down due to a car accident, and my husband died as a result of a head injury. All this before I was 40 years old. Many people never go through half of this in a lifetime. This lead to my addiction to tranquilizers and alcohol to avoid the reality and pain of it all, and to cope with life. But I knew there were other ways than this to a better way of life.

I slowly started to turn around every bit of the hell I was experiencing and I knew every tragedy I'd experienced that God could make it better if I allowed it. It was my choice. I am now 46 years old and somehow the past seems like it all belonged to someone else, like a book I'd read. My life blossomed and I wanted to share it with others. I decided to run for mayor of our small town of Browning, Montana, located in the center of the Blackfeet Reservation. The town had hit its bottom, too, and I knew the only way was up with the help of the Lord. Self-esteem was down; Browning had a poor image as far as the off-reservation cities were concerned. The work is to bring that stereotype image into a positive one, and I knew I could help. I believe in tithing time like money, you give to get. The rewards of giving are so much greater than receiving.

I am very fortunate I have two sons who support their mother enormously and are forever wondering what I am going to do next. Someday, I will be able to make up for all the hurt I've caused them. I feel I have a very full life of my own now for today, who knows what tomorrow will bring.

Kurt Wilson

FUNERAL DIRECTOR

Marion Judee Fluehr, 43, has been a funeral director for the past 15 years, and owns her own funeral home.

I was born and raised in Philadelphia, and am the daughter of a second generation funeral director. By the time I was 22 years old, I was a graduate of Temple University and Eckels College of Mortuary Science. I was one of two women in a class of 39 men. I took my apprenticeship under my father, who at the time owned two funeral homes. I became licensed, worked for my family, married and had two daughters. By the time I was 29, I was running my own funeral home, which we had just built in the Olney section of Philadelphia.

For the past 15 years I have owned and operated the funeral home in every respect. Making arrangements with the family, selling of the merchandise, dressing, cosmetology, hairdressing, conducting funerals and taking care of viewings. During the last few years I have seen more and more women entering this field, but only through family, marriage or death. Without family it is very difficult to make a good living as our area has no union in this business, and the pay scale is very poor. It is almost impossible to start your own business unless you are able to come up with almost a million dollars to build and get started.

The funeral business has had many rewards for me. It afforded me many luxuries materially, and also enabled me to work and have my children with me at all times, since we also lived at the funeral home. It has always given me a great feeling of satisfaction and a feeling of being helpful and useful at a most difficult time in someone's life. I have learned over the years that most people are more comfortable and are more at ease in speaking to and making arrangements with a woman. It is very gratifying to be able to make things easier on people and most helpful if you can put yourself in their position. I have learned much humility and compassion over the past 15 years.

As in everything, there are some negative sides to the business. In particular, your life is never your own, and believe me, this is a true statement. It is worse than a doctor. The phones and doorbell go 24 hours a day. You can never be sure of any hour of peace during any day if you want a personal relationship in this business, and in our area of hundreds of small funeral homes this is something you must have. The constant uncertainty of your time really gets to you. It is very hard on me and my family because they sometimes feel that business is always first. I lived this life with my father and have in my own personal relationships with my children tried to dispel this feeling.

In this day and age, being a woman and owning and running a full-time business does not help marriages . . . it is a great hindrance and I feel has been the downfall of my two marriages. When your life is working and making decisions constantly, it is very difficult for you to be the meek, docile wife who must ask permission or consult with your spouse about everything. Trying to be two people just doesn't work. Also, if you are making a greater income, this becomes a problem for some men to handle.

This is an excellent area for women to work in for it has been proven we are more compassionate with people and are much better in the merchandising area. If you can work a 40-hour week, it is a most rewarding business. I have advised my children not to enter the field unless they are employed by a funeral home for a 40-hour work week, enabling them to have more freedom to enjoy life itself, since we all know there is no guarantee there will be a tomorrow.

Linda Griffith

CUSTODIAN

Mattie Lou Bertha Banks, 43, has worked as a custodian for the past seven years at the Reynolds mansion in Georgia.

I'm a native of Sapelo Island, which is one of the barrier islands located on the coast of Georgia. I've lived here all of my life. I was raised by my great grandmother and was visited by my mother quite often. I attended high school in Brunswick, Georgia for two school terms, but I would always come back to the island at least twice a month to visit my family. No matter where I've went, I've never found any place like Sapelo, and could hardly wait to get back because Sapelo is such a nice place to live. I'm married and have six children and one grandchild.

One of the most important things about Sapelo to me is the two Baptist churches. Wherever I live or wherever I go, church will always be very important to me because wherever I am or wherever I go, I know I need God.

I've been employed by the University of Georgia Marine Institute on Sapelo Island for about seven years, and I like working there very much. My job title is Custodian I, and my work consists mostly of cleaning and laundering in the main house, a mansion where Richard J. Reynolds once lived. From time to time I also keep the brass polished, and just do whatever else I see that needs to be done to make guests that visit feel right at home. I don't have any dislikes about my job. I enjoy the type of work I do very much.

Bill Durrence

MIDWIVES

Gloria S. Riemenschneider, 60, and Jean Collins, 46, are Certified Nurse Midwives specializing in homebirths.

According to my mother, at an early age I talked of going into the mission field. I felt the call to serve God in the medical missions and graduated from Cornell University in 1949 with a Bachelor of Science in Nursing. When I found that I would be responsible for the obstetrical service in the small mission hospital to which I was assigned, I decided to study midwifery. In 1950, I graduated from the Maternity Center Association School of Nurse-Midwifery in New York City where my training was in homebirth.

After being in Iran 19 years, I returned to work in the labor and delivery area of local hospitals. I found the change in obstetrical practice both awing and appalling. I was awed by the technological advances and their uses, but at the same time, appalled by their misuse. I decided to start a homebirth service when an anesthesiologist who was upset by what he saw in hospital obstetrics asked me to help him and his wife have a safe homebirth. Researchers have shown that outcome in childbirth is not site related, but directly related to health of the mother, prenatal care, competency of the birth attendants, and appropriate use of technology. Many well educated women have chosen what, throughout history, has been the normal site for birth and remains so in much of the world today — the home.

At this point, midwives and obstetricians have polarized their groups, but it really need not be so. Obstetrical as well as family practice specialists have much to offer the midwives and the midwives have much to offer the specialists. The practices really complement one another; a close working relationship between them would certainly improve obstetrical care and outcome. Midwives and doctors in many countries have a close working, collaborative relationship no matter where the site of service. Why can't this be true in the United States where freedom of choice is one of our basic rights? According to the philosophy of the American College of Nurse-Midwives, every childbearing family has a right to a safe, satisfying experience with respect for human dignity and worth; for variety in cultural forms; and for the parents' right to self-determination.

Gloria

I never knew what I wanted to be. Remote relatives would ask and expect to have an answer, but at school's end and at the age of 17, I still did not have one. It did not take many days behind a desk for me to decide that wasn't for me, so on my 18th birthday I became a student nurse. In England, it is customary for qualified nurses (who are called State Registered Nurses) to continue their education and specialize in a field of their choice. I chose midwifery and have not regretted my choice.

I landed in the "New World" in 1962 and felt I had taken a step back in time after leaving a country that helped women have babies in their own homes amongst their loved ones. I found myself "helping" women by giving them I.V. injections of scopolomine and restraining them in their beds with side rails and sometimes strapping their hands down. These women would deliver, and maybe two hours later would see their baby. Twenty years later we have come full cycle. Yes, now we truly help mothers have their babies together with family, alert, participating in the birth experience, encouraging involvement and preparation. We can do more . . . many new mothers are not aware of the services available through Certified Nurse Midwives and the dedicated care and educational experience which they offer as an alternative way to have a baby, which is a *natural* process.

Being a nurse-midwife in America is always to be fighting. Fighting for the right to assist parents in a natural process, because some in the medical profession want to make it an unnatural process and invade the maternal body and fetus for tests and procedures. Fighting to stay in the profession without feeling that every day may be your last because an insurance company cannot be found willing to back nurse-midwives as liability coverage.

Midwifery is a profession of extreme emotions; it is working with women and their families to guide them, encourage them and initiate them in the intricacies of childbirth. It is my wish for every pregnant woman I come in contact with to have the most joyous, wonderful obstetrical experience possible. The disappointment in this profession is that obviously, not everyone meets this goal.

Jean

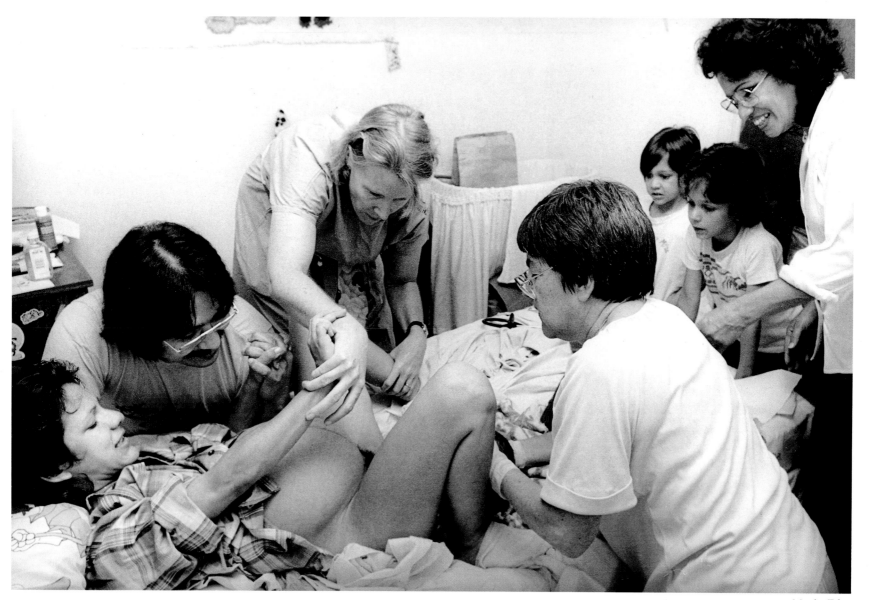

Martha Tabor

CABINETMAKER

Sandra Marilyn, 40, is an industrial cabinetmaker and the only
woman in a union of 900 men.

As were most girls growing up in the 1950's in middle America,
I was strongly encouraged to slide neatly into one of the
well-worn grooves that tradition had made for women. Although my
socialization to be a proper lady with a proper lady's job had a
mighty pull, there were other influences which did not come to the
front for many years. My mother, who was an art teacher, had
strong opinions about the importance of craftswomen in the scope
of what we call art, and felt that as much artistic value could be
given to something that was made to be used, as to something that
was only made to be hung on a wall.

In my late 20s my desire to work with my hands, and to contribute
useful and beautiful things to the world, won out over my desire to
be a proper lady with a proper lady's job. I began my struggle to
find a place for myself in the male-dominated field of cabinetmaking
in Austin, Texas. After many stops and starts, and enough successes
to keep me fighting for more, I moved to California to continue the
battle in what I hoped would be a more progressive place.

In San Francisco, I obtained a union apprenticeship only to find out
on my first day of work that there were no other women in the
union of 900 men. Although California did not prove to be more
progressive than Texas, I was encouraged by the many powerful
and brave women I met who were trying to make new traditions for
women. Now, in 1986, I am the first journeywoman cabinetmaker in
Mill Cabinet Local #42 of the United Brotherhood of Carpenters
and Joiners of America, and there are still no other women in the
union.

Ann Meredith

WHALE RESEARCHER

Deborah Glockner-Ferrari, 35, is Director of Humpback Whale Research at the California Marine Mammal Center, and a pioneer in underwater study of the humpback, a critically endangered species. At one time, she worked as a waitress nights to support her daytime research, and in the off season, an assortment of odd jobs. Recently, she has begun to receive grant money for her research.

From atop the ocean's surface, I peered through my mask into the depths below. About 50 feet beneath me, a humpback whale mother and calf lay motionless. Excitedly, I photographed their greyish-black flippers and the calf's tiny white chin and mottled belly. Gradually, the calf began to rise. As it approached within several feet of my camera, I quickly counted the lip grooves below its mouth. They numbered three. I had previously found that the lip groove pattern could be used to identify each whale, the pattern being unique to the individual, much like human fingerprints. I then noted that the young calf was a male. With his eyes opened wide, he watched me as I observed him. The calf didn't have any fear at all. He spouted at the surface three times in a row, swimming in a small clockwise circle. Then, he sounded, diving down towards his mother.

Several minutes passed by. The mother and calf rose together, spouting in unison. The calf playfully twirled its body and began to swim upside down. His eyes were now closed. The mother gently touched her calf with her flippers. Slowly, they descended into the depths below. A feeling of peacefulness pervaded the waters . . .

To the beauty of nature itself and to an absolutely wonderful family, I owe my love of whales and dolphins. Born in New Orleans, I grew up in Louisiana in a beautiful little town called Covington that nestled amidst flowering woodlands along the winding Bogue Falaya and Tchefuncte Rivers. I graduated in 1972 from Louisiana State University with a Bachelor of Science degree in Biochemistry. After working in this field for a while, I began practicing transcendental meditation (TM). As TM became an integral part of my life, my heart opened even more to seeing the beauty of wildlife and all of nature. I obtained a summer job at an oceanarium in Gulfport, Mississippi, as a dolphin trainer, followed by a lab assistant position at the University of Hawaii dolphin lab. In 1975, I had my first opportunity to observe a humpback whale mother and calf underwater. I knew then that I

wanted to study whales and dolphins in their natural environment as my lifetime work.

I began an annual study of humpback whales in the waters off the west coast of Maui, Hawaii. Using benign photographic techniques, I began identifying individual whales, especially mothers and calves by the color pattern of the lip grooves, the shape of the dorsal fin, and any unusual scarring. Using a 15½- foot inflatable Zodiac to slowly motor to the area in which whales are located, I'd gently enter the water with only snorkeling equipment and camera gear to make underwater observations and identifications. I soon found that I was able to track individual whales over successive years. In 1979, I discovered a simple technique to determine the sex of a whale by observing the lateral or ventral view of the whale for the presence of a lobe found only in females. Through identifying known mothers and calves over successive years, I was able to determine that some females had an unexpectedly high reproductive rate and were capable of producing calves annually.

In 1980 my husband, Mark Ferrari, a sensitive, and talented wildlife photographer, joined the project. The study focuses on the identification, behavior, reproduction, and distribution of humpback whales, and observations of interactions between whales and boats. We discovered that the percentage of humpback whale mothers and calves resting in nearshore waters was decreasing dramatically each year as high speed, nearshore activities were increasing and the water quality decreasing. As our concern mounted, we expanded the project to include an education program. We are planning to continue our long term study and are hoping to influence regulations to protect humpback whales and aid in establishing a Critical Habitat in the waters surrounding the Hawaiian Islands to further the survival of this endangered species. Our project is supported by Wildlife Conservation International, World Wildlife Fund, and Maui Whale Watchers.

Photos: Mark Ferrari

MEDICAL RECORDS CLERK

Susan Bernadette Pedrick, 27, is a medical records clerk at a hospital.

Writing about my employment is no small can of worms. In order to appreciate how I pay rent, an explanation of the events leading to my job would be very high in order. The saga of my employment begins when I was fresh out of high school and a girls' group home and I was hired by the phone company as a directory assistance operator in 1976. For two-and-a-half years I endured the purgatory of giving out 900 telephone numbers a day until I was graciously granted a transfer to plant services where I stayed five years.

It doesn't really matter what I did or where I worked, what matters is that everywhere I went, people rather enthusiastically liked or disliked me. That, and the fact that my lifestyle changed drastically to a degree that profoundly affected its end. In short, I started using a lot of drugs. Eventually, the phone company reminded me that I was not the same person they had hired five years previously and invited me to leave, which I did without a fight in 1981. I forgive myself for this and don't regret it. Mainly because I needed to get a lot of things out of my system and it was becoming increasingly more difficult to integrate with a full-time job in an environment like that of a large utility company.

Painful and dark things in 1982 led to two incarcerations and three trips to the hospital. However, at the end of that year I had had enough. I had created as many creepy environments and contrived as many paradoxically unfortunate circumstances for myself as I was ultimately capable of producing or enduring. I decided to start putting one foot in front of the other and dig myself out of the hole I had taken such care to prepare. So, in January of 1983 I started working as a temporary with an agency. My typing skills were not exactly impeccable, so it was desperately long before the agency found me an assignment. I was the sort of "temp" whose entire income consisted of whatever the agency could come up with for me, and after about a week-and-a-half without work, I panicked. I looked into being a leaflet distributor and ended up enduring seven hours on a truck and managed to earn all of $7.50.

On days that my agency didn't have work for me, often I dressed anyway and went down in person which, if nothing else, certainly left the agency with an impression of me as a motivated, dependable person. Finally, one Friday afternoon in January 1984, it was getting down to the wire on whether or not the agency would have work for me Monday morning. At long last they called and said they had an assignment, but apologized because it was not downtown. It turned out to be working at a hospital eight blocks from where I live!

When I got to the hospital, I encountered an environment that seemed as though if I were ambitious enough it could turn into permanent work. I think I was making $5.50 an hour, which was peak for me. I was thrilled, and I worked very hard making sure the powers that be were aware of this. I found myself surrounded by people who complained constantly, which appalled me because a large percentage of them were making nearly twice as much as I had struggled to make at other jobs. About four months into my assignment, I was offered a full time job which meant an instant *$500 a month raise and benefits*.

In short, considering that I had gone as far as entering amateur stripping contests in nude theaters — and winning them — I'd have to say the thing I like most about my job is *having* it. Other than that, I appreciate working for a hospital and not a utility or oil company. I thoroughly enjoy being on the positive end and helping people who are in real and dire need of the services I provide. I may only be in medical records, but sometimes what I can do for people is almost as beneficial to them as anything a doctor could do and I am very thankful that I accidentally wound up in such an uplifting context. On the other hand, I envy the people who were getting college educations while I really had no choice but to fight an exhausting war between my ears as a result of a history that is a little more colorful than I care for it to have been. So, my pet peeve is the fate of being bossed around by people of questionable intelligence simply because they were able to get credentials while I was forced to clean up a mess I didn't make. But I am closer than ever to winning that war and cleaning up that mess. In fact, I may be about to flip the switch from a career of trying to stay out of trouble to getting my first promotion. Wish me luck.

Nita Winter

CHILDCARE WORKER

Celene Ostlund, 20, works at a childcare center.

I am the fourth child and the second girl in a family of nine children. At 13, I was the oldest girl still at home, so, along with my 11-year-old sister, I took on the responsibility for the last baby, Karen, as well as my three-year-old sister, and five-year-old brother. Even before they were born, I had always loved children. My earliest memories are of begging mothers to have their babies on my lap at every social gathering.

While I was growing up, there was never a dull moment in my house. Whether it was kids yelling, doors slamming or toilets flushing, *big* noise was the rule. With all those people around, you never had to worry about being lonely because there was always something going on. Maybe that's why I don't seem to mind the 12 babies, six weeks to 18 months old, that I work with at the children's center.

Lunch time is always pure chaos. Of course, all 12 babies want to eat at the same time, and they all start screaming at once. It reminds me of home. I can see my mother now, feeding three or four lined up on the floor, another few in high chairs, and all the while talking on the telephone. She did it, and so can I.

In my junior year of high school I started working at the children's center as an aide. To me, it is a most rewarding kind of job. Several children have become attached to me in a special kind of way. When I first started, the twins Katie and Jennifer, were six months old and just starting, too. Now, they're two and call me "Aunt" Celene. You can't get that kind of pay in any other job.

Gary McCarthy

BURN WARD NURSES

Cynthia L. Bennett, 29, and Debra Lynn Henderson, 30, (nurse to the right in photo) are registered nurses at the Akron Children's Hospital Regional Burn Center in Ohio.

Working at the Burn Center has been both an enriching and enlightening experience. The horrors and depressing atmosphere associated with a burn center are minor in comparison with the personal satisfaction I've attained while working there. Many times a personal problem or concern becomes minute while handling or listening to a burn patient's suffering. It is very rewarding to be appreciated for providing compassion, a simple human service.

I had never dreamed I'd become a burn nurse. Now, after nearly nine years, it was obviously meant to be. After nursing school I'd chosen to work at Children's Hospital. There were only two openings; newborn intensive care and burn center. After considering the diversity a burn center could offer, the choice was easy. The idea itself scared me to death, but I kept one thought in mind: "If I can work there, I can work anywhere!" This has turned out to be *so* true. Managing to keep my sanity and productivity over these years has been a challenge. I'm sure this experience has enhanced every facet of my life. I began nursing when I was very young and emotionally immature. I've since grown immeasurably while counseling, teaching, or sometimes just holding a patient or family member.

The major drawback to working in a burn center is finding a constructive way to release pent up emotions. Believe me, this is a priority! I have found daily naps and weekly church visits seem to help. I often rely on physical activity in the form of sports as a release. Sporting events used to be the greatest challenge of my life, but without a doubt, nursing is a far greater challenge. Maintaining the high standards of care and professional morality I've learned both at home and in nursing school, is no easy task. Much of the guidance I've received in nursing was provided by my mother, a nurse for 33 years now, who has been a fine example and a great inspiration.

Cynthia

Being a registered nurse for seven years now, I really do love my job, but this was no lifelong dream. As a matter of fact, two years into college, I was still unsure of my goals. You could say I was one of the luckier ones, my dad was putting me through college so there was no hurry. I had always been encouraged by my parents to get a degree in something I could use to support myself. My dad always said, "Never be dependent on anyone." I was attending Kent State University, so I researched the Nursing Department and graduated four years later with a degree in nursing.

After working in the burn center, I feel as though I could handle any aspect of nursing. Along with burns come trauma, surgery and an array of medical problems. I enjoy the challenge that a serious burn can present. Burns can affect just about every system of the body and things can become quite complex. Our burn center treats adults and children of all ages. Adults are easier for me to deal with because they understand the "whys" of treatment. Children just look at you like, "Why are you hurting me?" It's especially hard for me because I have a four-year-old boy at home, and we do get child abuse cases, but few and far between, thank goodness.

I don't care for the hours and that I have to work weekends. And I don't particularly like leaving my son with a sitter 50 hours a week. He's in preschool now, so it's not so bad. I guess it's the price any working mother has to pay. I spend "quality" time with Nathan and my new husband (I remarried in December). Now that I'm expecting my second baby, I hope to go part-time for a few years. My husband will be graduating in May from Kent State with his nursing degree. I really feel as though I could work with burn patients for a long time.

Debra

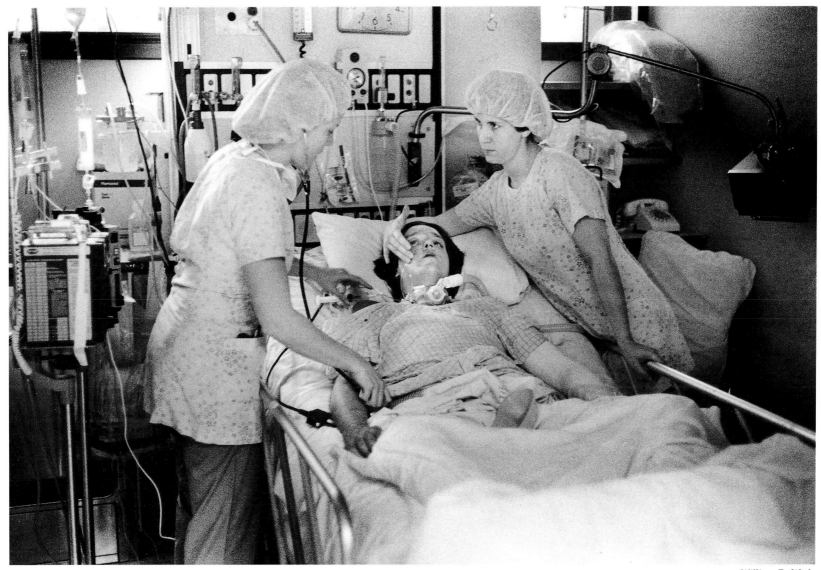

William D. Wade

SCULPTOR

Karin F. Giusti, 30, is a sculptor.

I think there can be no other profession that is such a blend of fact and fiction. On one hand you are expected to be the latest diva on the art scene and on the other hand, nuts and bolts, machine oil and welding equipment proliferate your environment. Most of what people see of my sculptures are at openings or in collections when the pieces are in their finished forms. The work in progress is what mystifies me — the metamorphosis of a piece. In their cocoon stages, the sculptures can be very homely and I must work many hours sanding, scraping, hammering, doing very physical labor with just a vision in my mind of what the emerging piece will look like. It is at this pupa stage where I believe there is a transference of life blood or spirit. In this respect, I feel that my work is different from other working experiences because it is such an extension of myself — like a birthing experience — painful and euphoric all at once.

My time out of the studio is spent foraging for materials in the junk yards, house-wrecking companies, hardware stores and welding shops. At first, I'm always an oddity to the people who work at these establishments because of the few women they see in their working day. Also, usually having just come from my studio, I'm pretty dirty and in this society there is a stigma about using one's hands to work and getting dirty, especially for a woman. Yet, I'm proud of my artistic skills, partly because they were so hard to come by.

I think that many women have been trained to be afraid of tools as dangerous objects that they can hurt themselves with. I found that when I was studying sculpture at one particular university, the fear was used to keep females out of the way in an overcrowded studio space. I compensated for that by working as a construction and shop welder while acquiring my Bachelor of Fine Arts degree.

For the several years I worked as a welder I never saw another woman on the job. Even though I had planned to keep welding on the side, the experience proved to be too isolating, so I decided to work exclusively on developing my art.

Now that I've been practicing in my field for a number of years, I realize how fortunate I am to be doing something I love to do and that I'm committed to. But I'd have to admit if I had a child who wanted to become an artist, I would not be very pleased. This is because surviving in this career is extremely difficult. Not only must you be a shrewd and aggressive business person, but you must keep sacred that other part of you that houses the spiritual and creative processes. With all things considered, I think it's all been worth it.

Nancy Palmieri

PEACE WORKER

Justine Merritt, 62, initiated The Ribbon project in 1982 which was comprised of 25,000 pieces created by thousands of people supporting a world without nuclear weapons. In 1985, The Ribbon was tied around the Pentagon in Washington, D.C.

Like countless other women, I went back to "work" as five children grew older and college beckoned to the first. I went into teaching to help with tuition costs and discovered I loved teaching. After years of cookies, cakes, a modest garden and some sewing, I discovered in lesson plan and classroom dynamics a splendid outlet for my creative energy. A few years later I resigned from the job I loved because of the blatant racism in the nation (two Black Panthers had been murdered in Chicago) deciding that I needed to work in the field of human relations. Within the supportive group of friends in the small agency where I was a volunteer, I found the support to sustain me as I sought a divorce after 25 years of marriage.

Numerous small jobs along the way, and travels that took me to Japan and Africa, prepared me for the kind of organizing necessary to help "The Ribbon" project to unwind. And when people ask, "How did you ever think of such an idea?" I tell them I went on a silent retreat in February of 1982, trying to discern the next journey — and I was praying. After running away from the peace movement for 37 years, I discovered in prayer that I was called to work for peace, and The Ribbon grew out of that call. It occurred to me to tie a ribbon around the Pentagon, envisioning the ribbon as a symbol of peace encircling a symbol of war. It would be tied around the Pentagon in August of 1985, the 40th anniversary of the bombings of Hiroshima and Nagasaki.

From its conception in 1982, The Ribbon called remarkable women to become involved in a project some have called folk art, others "lifesaving." For four years I traveled, talking about the need to face the reality of living in a nuclear age, and then offering the listeners an opportunity to create on fabric a symbol of what they "cannot bear to think of as lost forever in a nuclear war." The time people spent thinking of an appropriate symbol and then creating it, released a promise for the future in its affirmation of life . . . one that had been buried beneath apathy, fear and pain. I faced the reality that the lives of my grandchildren are in jeopardy, every shell, flower and bird are in jeopardy and that nuclear weapons make each one an endangered species.

Many women discovered new skills of organizing as well as old skills of embroidery and quilting and were affirmed as both leaders and artists. Women wrote songs and poems, photographed local events, stayed up late nights putting together mailing lists and treasurer's reports. I found members of the board, including my mother and old friends. Mary Frances Jaster, the National Coordinator, found the 50 state coordinators, and they in turn, found 50, 500, 1500 volunteers. And so, the idea grew. Everywhere there are compassionate and intelligent people working for peace and this foolish idea, to tie The Ribbon around the Pentagon, created an international network.

On August 4, 1985, we carried The Ribbon around the Pentagon and stretched down the freeway, crossed Memorial Bridge, past the Lincoln Memorial, along the reflecting pool, around the elipse behind the White House, up and around the Capitol and back again. Ten miles of joy-filled humans, some in baby strollers and some in wheelchairs, carrying some of the 25,000 segments created by caring people around the globe. The people who created Ribbon segments, and the people who came to the August event represented widely divergent religious, political, and economic backgrounds as well as every age and color. Organized by women from the Center for New Creation in Arlington, Virginia, The Ribbon unwound with order and beauty.

I discovered along the journey that I am a workaholic and some of my friends are too . . . but there are times when the energy and the need combine to get the job done. Thousands of us tied a ribbon around the Pentagon because we love the earth and all its people. We honored our diversity; we celebrated our unity as we worked together to gently lead our leaders on the road to peace.

Martha Tabor

WIFE & DAUGHTER

Jo Anne Stanley, 64, was married 39 years when her husband Ben was diagnosed with lung cancer. With the help of their daughter, Brooke Simon, 33, Jo Anne cared for Ben in his final months. Ben approved of a photographer to chronicle the end of his journey, up to the final hour as he took his last sips of nourishment, and as his wife and daughter realized his death.

About Daddy. In the beginning, we wrestled with the doctors' views. They said two months to live, a giant tumor in the left lung. Surgery could be performed, but Daddy wouldn't go, so we decided on hospice. Mom wanted him to be with her. We all wanted to help, but we wanted to know: What would the last day be like? As a nurse, I had seen death many times — before, during and after, but still the same fear nagged at us . . . what would the actual death be like? His dying was not a job for me or a labor in anyway. It was a time we knew we had to become closer, share feelings and just love each other. One doctor had a good bit of advice: "It doesn't matter what happens, just *be there*." So a lot of days I was just there. I was numbed by his physical decline and the acute pain that he was having. But for so long he was himself — feisty, wise and loving — that the last three days I really wasn't prepared to lose him.

On the day of his death, I'll never forget my two-year-old daughter, Hayley, singing . . . she walked around singing in an angel's voice. Daddy and I knew it was a premonition. He held our hands and patted them especially that day; he would always pat with his beautiful, big hands, the fingers slender and strong. There was always a heaviness of love in his hands. As he was dying that last day I decided to tell him my feelings before he died. After Hayley's song, I was so touched I began to cry. That was when I asked him, "Why did you have to love us that much?" It was too much to keep inside. I mentioned everything I could think of that he did for us and with us. He just kept patting my hand, but his body was bent over from the waist and his eyes swollen shut. I knew that he heard me and understood.

Daddy was calm the day he died. He would answer our questions with a nod of the head or a short reply. He was resting intermittently, but awfully restless. I decided to call the doctor. When I re-entered the bedroom, he was already gone. It was terrible, but it was over. His suffering was over and in that we were united in joy.

When Ben was diagnosed with cancer of the lungs in 1985, we decided to be together, at home, and we found that hospice would help us do this. The doctor said three months, so hospice assigned a visitor and a nurse, also a counselor. Ben began painting, and writing answers to all the letters that started to come in. We played gin rummy whenever I needed a break, and he was always ready to talk and play and laugh a little. We decided the children should come and visit, one at a time. I wondered how hard those visits were for Ben, but hospice said they were "business to be attended to."

We did wills, etcetera. Ben began writing investment advice to me in letter form plus a continuing love letter full of memories . . . I was to read this after he died. We had many late night talks about our high and low points together. I shuffled guests in and out, even a newspaper reporter and photographer. Ben was in surprisingly good health, but tired easily and took a lot of naps. My daughter Brooke, a nurse, came to help with baths three times a week. I'd usually go out with my granddaughter, three-year-old Hayley, for a walk and visit, sometimes a swim. These little breaks were real lifesavers. As food lost its attraction, we worked together to develop a sort of smorgasbord for dinner time. It's hard to think of all this as caregiving — I was his other half; what the opposite half needed done, I did.

About March 20th my daughter came to be with her dad again, and had me get away for an overnight at a friend's house. I came home somewhat refreshed and within two or three days, Ben seemed to turn a corner — we went around it together. We didn't eat much — talked a little — smiled at each other often. On Tuesday or Wednesday night, Brooke and I each took turns — Ben slid back and forth into consciousness. Thursday morning, I talked to the hospice nurse and asked her to come and assess things. She inserted a catheter and said she didn't think Ben had long.

As I sat beside Ben around 3 p.m. — the room was full of sunshine, windows open, Hayley playing quietly nearby — I asked him something. He closed his eyes, thinking of an answer — he stopped breathing. I just accepted this — this is what we'd both worked four months to achieve. How can I grieve — he's still not very far away.

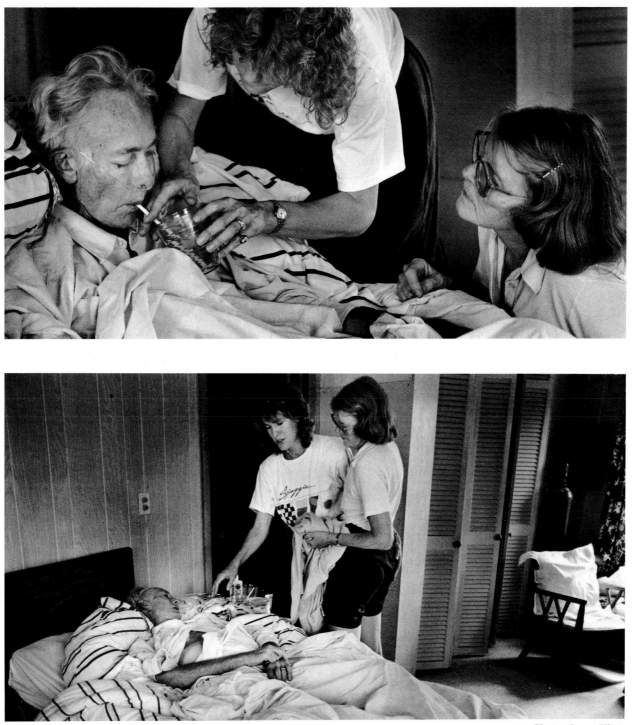

Photos: Laura Elliott

BALLET DANCER

Suzanne Goldman, 24, has been a ballet dancer since she was seven years old, at one time performing with the American Ballet Theatre.

To start at the top of your chosen field is not often a possibility. Some may believe it is an instant pathway to glory. For me, it was a disillusioning experience — one which forced me to reevaluate my goals and begin again a career I had chosen to pursue when I was only seven years old.

I began to study ballet at the famous School of American Ballet in New York City, appearing in all the New York City Ballet productions that used small children like "The Nutcracker," "Circus Polka," and "Midsummer's Night Dream." At 13, I was offered a scholarship at the American Ballet Theatre School (ABT), then under the direction of Lucia Chase. It had always been my dream to be a member of that company, and at the age of 17 I was accepted into the corps de ballet — a professional ballet dancer.

Most of my peers would have sold their souls to achieve what I had achieved at such a young age — to be a part of this prestigious company. In a way, I sold my soul to this company which I discovered not too soon afterwards, had very little time for me. Because of the size, scope, and popularity of the company, and because Mikhail Baryshnikov had just assumed directorship, the focus of the company changed. I was given no time to develop as an artist.

After devoting ten years of my life to the difficult, demanding training, living in an isolated existence of physical exertion, and seeking only perfection of the body, my spirit began to wane. Working in the daily work atmosphere of ABT amongst those who cared not to nurture or protect its young dancers, my motivation dwindled and almost completely ceased to exist. After six years of being a Ballet Theatre dancer, I left and came to San Francisco to rethink my life.

First, I met a stimulating, gifted teacher, and began to take some classes with him. Then I performed occasionally with the Oakland Ballet under the guidance of a thoughtful director. Soon, I realized I was beginning to perfect my technique in new and exciting ways and performing with a new-found confidence. Slowly, the pressure and discontentment of my early years on stage eased. Now I feel once more reassured and confident, certain that I will fulfill those early goals of my life . . . all those aspirations and dreams that inspired me to begin my life as a ballerina.

Niki Berg

VETERINARIAN

Alice Villalobos, 39, is a veterinarian specializing in the treatment and clinical research of cancer in pet animals.

I was either going to be a nun or a veterinarian since the 3rd grade, but since there were no convents offering veterinary medical training, after graduation from St. Mary's, I chose to pursue my scientific career as a worldly individual, attending El Camino Junior College in the South Bay of Los Angeles, Long Beach State, and then U.C. Davis. I remember each step of the way as a struggle with great personal rewards. Very few counsellors, family members or teachers really encouraged me at the beginning and I don't blame them. Truly, getting into U.C. Davis vet school in 1966, 1967 and 1968 was a chance of 12.5 to 1 — and worse for females! It took me three applications to get in.

It was harder preparing and trying to get into vet school than being in it. For one thing, money. Once I got in, the health professions loans were forthcoming. Being number four in a family of five children, with my dad working in a factory all his life for $6,000 a year and just being laid off, wasn't exactly predicting my destiny. Everyone started to believe in me once I got into veterinary school.

Life has continued to be a struggle with great personal rewards on a daily basis. Struggles, rewards and losses because I'm not practicing general veterinary medicine as most members of my profession do. Early on in my career, I decided to specialize in cancer therapy for pets. This obsession lead to the start of my own clinic in order to have the freedom of a 45-minute office call, rather than the routine 10-to-15-minute type. Now, apparently I have ownership of probably the largest veterinary facility owned by a "single woman," as the law states it.

I've been involved in the field of cancer research for 15 years and I'm considered a grandmother in the field, a world reknowned expert in diseases related to cancer, such as feline leukemia virus. I've never seen so much interest in animal cancer as I have in the last two years. We're giving clients an advantage to fight tumorous cancers in a more advanced way than what is accepted now for humans. I have

five outstanding women veterinarians as associates, comprising our "six man" practice. There are six top-notch women who are California licensed Animal Health Technicians, and with our support staff, we total 35 people who are very prepared, interested and committed in the care of man's best friend.

Among our patients are what I call "victims of our cement society" which is encroaching on wilderness animals such as the possum who was hit by a car. We provide medical care for homeless, wild, injured or sick animals through a fund set up to accept donations from the kind-hearted and from our hospital directing all fees for euthanasia towards the fund. Besides caring for cancer patients referred to our service from veterinarians all over Southern California, we place 250 to 300 kittens and aid about 175 birds and other miscellaneous animals on a yearly basis.

Every day has its struggles. My biggest headache is the responsibilities of keeping a service-oriented business operational. Preserving the love relationship that forms between people and pets is where my heart is and just a sincere "thank you, doc" for helping "my little pal" is our reward.

Brad Graverson

CONCERT PIANIST

Johana Harris-Heggie, 73, is a concert pianist whose lifetime of work in the music world rates her among world-class artists. In addition to a steady stream of performances, she is also on the faculty at the University of California, Los Angeles, Music Department.

I was born to be in music. At the age of two, and for all the years since, playing the piano has been great fun. My family was not musical, but there were pianos in the households, and that is where I felt most at home. I was never discouraged, nor on the other hand fortunately, "pushed." I attended private schools and was given the best musical training at the Canadian Conservatory in Ottawa, probably beginning at age 5, because I performed in recitals soon thereafter, and have been performing in public ever since. Blessed with a "good ear" (perfect pitch), playing "by ear" is fun to this day. It seems to please people to hear an improvisation or medley on dozens of "favorites" all woven together.

As a child, I was very healthy. I skated, ran lots of races, danced a great deal, and made mud pies! My general education was superior, and reading fine books remains one of my most cherished occupations, but *not* books on music. I like to hear it and perform it, rather than read about it. By age ten I had heard wonderful musicians perform and was in a Master Class with adults who were stunning pianists. It was agreed that New York City was where I belonged, so my family took me there. I auditioned and won scholarships in piano with Ernest Hutcheson and composition with Reuben Goldmark at the Juilliard School at the age of 12, and by the time I was 15, I began teaching, becoming the youngest faculty member in Juilliard's history. Always believing in being well rounded in the field, I studied voice, viola, and was a professional dancer for ten years. I had a vocal scholarship in Berlin as a young girl and had lessons daily with the favorite court singer of the Kaiser. But I felt most at home at a keyboard.

At Juilliard I met the American composer Roy Harris, and we were married in 1936. I illustrated his lectures on the 48 Preludes and Fugues of Bach, and recorded for the State Department the 32 Beethoven Piano Sonatas, all of the piano and violin sonatas, the cello and piano sonatas, and the trios with the first chair players of the Pittsburgh Symphony. Through all the years I have had the privilege of performing with orchestras, chamber groups, in solo recitals, and in collaboration with many of the world's greatest artists: William Primrose, Josef Gingold, Janos Starker, and Yehudi Menuhin, to name a few.

Some of the lighter times in New York City occurred when I played for fun with Tommy Dorsey and Larry Adler, and more seriously, chamber music with Benny Goodman. The old Algonquin Hotel in New York was a favorite meeting place for writers and this period was very nourishing; and to have poets write special poetry as send off gifts on sailing for Europe was always a highlight in living. Playing duets with Norman Cousins whom I admire wholeheartedly and accompanying Arthur Miller singing at parties — these were fun times. Improvising duets with Samuel Barber was a highlight. Frank Lloyd Wright and Robert Frost were friends, and Ben Spock called me up to ask what he should do with his own kids!

Making music with other performers is very much like any first-class teamwork in athletics. It is a responsibility to share all the human emotions represented through the ages in music, to serve the church, the courts, the large general public and smaller chamber music clientele for fun and games and dancing and for funerals. It has been an honor to present the world premiere performances of many works, including all the Harris works involving piano. Most gratifying in my life has been the giving of benefit concerts for causes in which I believe, such as scholarship aid for worthy students, funds to babies, and housing for hurricane victims in Puerto Rico. Giving Red Cross Benefit Concerts for Canada during the war made me feel proud. I have been nominated for the Wolf Foundation Prize from Israel for "outstanding achievement for the benefit of humanity and brotherly relations amongst the peoples; regardless of nationality, race, color, religion, sex, or political views."

I believe in a God-given gift, for which one can take no credit. There is no explaining how a youngster can move people to tears or great jubilation through the performing of music. It is an awesome experience. As years accumulate, and playing continues to be the greatest joy as one learns about the whole history of the art and the geniuses who composed vast amounts of great music, the performer very humbly acknowledges a huge, challenging responsibility and accepts the disciplines required to improve and enlarge equipment to be worthy of our history and serve the public with dignity.

I was blessed with wonderful health and eager energy. I had five children, and now four grandchildren. I performed and taught through each pregnancy — fancy flouncy gowns hide a lot! Typical working days could be all the daily duties of meals, laundry, housekeeping, teaching, rehearsing, being a den mother, playing with the children, rubbing backs and singing folksongs to them. Our home has housed and helped dozens of young musicians and composers and is always a meeting place for artists and writers as well. Folk singers flocked to our house and we swapped innumerable songs. Burl Ives, Alan Lomax and John Jacob Niles were like part of the family. During the war, my job was singing folksongs through the Office of War Information for our men in the foxholes.

I have taught at Juilliard, Princeton, the Westminster Choir School, Cornell University and Cambridge University in England, among others. For the past 17 years I have taught at UCLA, and this spring won the Distinguished Teaching Award. For my nature, the academic world holds too many meetings, memos, and at times poor students, calling on patience, humor, imagination and compassion, resulting in exhaustion because I cannot utilize my expertise, musical vocabulary, or experience that I have been trained to share, nor feel the exuberance nurtured by achievement. Being a good teacher demands so much more than sharing the field in which one specializes. Upholding standards in human behavior, vocabulary and grace and standing for the dignity so needed in human relations are a few needs. The gratifications arise from students who carry on and become serviceable accompanists, church musicians, chamber players, and sometimes great soloists and very good teachers.

In 1979 my husband, Roy Harris, died, and in 1982 I married my gifted student Jake Heggie. He is a first-class composer, pianist, and artist. We are a two-piano team that is referred to as "magic." That's fabulous fun! We have a glorious life together. On ending this incomplete story I amused myself by making three long columns of overlooked information. But it had to stop someplace and it is clear, life leaps on vigorously.

Claire Rydell

STREET VENDOR

Maria, 35, is a Salvadoran refugee who came to the United States to flee the war in her homeland, El Salvador, a small country in Central America where thousands of innocent people have died because of the war within that country. Maria is one of an estimated 300,000 Salvadoran refugees living in Los Angeles, and some 500,000 nationwide who have fled their country seeking sanctuary and political refuge. She told her story in Spanish to the photographer.

Everyday, seven days a week, Maria sells her wares on the downtown streets of Los Angeles, "Un dolar! One dollar!" Oftentimes for 11 hours a day she stands behind a box of socks, women's underwear and cosmetics, each of which sells for about a dollar, hawking her wares and earning 25¢ to the dollar. During rainy weather she sells umbrellas. "I make about $100 a week as a street vendor when sales are good, and from this I must pay for food, rent and transportation to work." She doesn't complain, just tells her story. It is clear she is willing to work hard.

Maria left El Salvador after her nephew and brother-in-law had been killed by the government's National Guard. Her brother-in-law had been a union representative in the factory where he worked, and was killed for his organizing activities. "He was the strongest one in the family. His death hit us hard." She had to leave behind her 13-year-old son to be cared for by her widowed sister who also has children. One day she hopes to bring her son to the United States. But so far, she has only been able to send $200 for her son, and she still owes money to the people in El Salvador who lent her money to leave the country. She misses her family, but does not plan to go back: "Life is hard and it is dangerous."

Maria has always been a vendor. While living in El Salvador, she sold chickens in the marketplace along with eggs laid by hens raised in the country. During the time she has been in the United States, Maria has had other jobs, among them cleaning offices 12 hours a day. But that job ended when the owner of the company never paid her $279

for her work — "He declared bankruptcy," Maria explains, although it is clear she knows this was not the truth. Next, she found a job selling newspapers and magazines, and then Spanish publications to passers-by. But the city government soon made a sweep of the street vendors, and along with many other women, she was left without even the small wooden box she had used as her chair.

Since she is often sick, Maria would like to get a medical exam, she thinks she may have diabetes. She can barely see with her right eye and knows it is getting worse. Never having gone to school, she can read very little Spanish, but the letter she was given by the medical clinic is only in English. She hopes she may be able to get care in a few months. At times, she is depressed: "Life is very hard here, but I know I must keep on." She is sad to be so far away from her family, but along with the other women vendors, she laughs and banters as if they had no cares in the world. Sons come to sit with some of them; friends or family often bring water or advance warning of an approaching police car. One would never know the sadness and tragedy behind the faces of this downtown street community.

Alberto Oropeza

JOCKEY

Patricia J. Cooksey, 28, has been the leading female jockey five of the last six years, and in the top ten percent of all male riders nationwide. She was the second woman to race in the Kentucky Derby, and the first female jockey to ride in the Preakness Stakes in 1985. Her winnings include several "stakes" worth more than $100,000.

When I was growing up with three older brothers and one younger sister, I didn't play with dolls, but instead played trucks, football and war with my brothers. I was a true tomboy! Throughout high school, I participated in track, basketball, softball and lettered in all three sports. I went to the University of Akron in Ohio, really just to play on the basketball team and be in the band. I was to major in Criminal Justice Technology because I wanted to be a cop! Am I ever glad they had a height requirement for police work. At 4'7", I was advised to take up a different profession. I was at the crossroads of my life when by chance, a friend arranged a job for me as a hot walker and groom for horses making $75 per week, before taxes. So, I packed up my car with my dog and headed for West Virginia. I was an excellent groom and very conscientious about all the horses. I was going to be a race rider! In order to strengthen my arms, I shoveled manure and carried water buckets.

For two years I groomed and galloped horses until my first race in August of 1979. My first mount was one never to be forgotten. I was nervous, but excited at the same time. The whole backside personnel came to watch the "new girl rider." My horse ran last, my legs didn't want to hold me up after the race, and everyone was saying, "She'd never make it." That's when I said, "Watch me!" I won with my second mount I rode and it's been an uphill climb ever since. I'm a good jockey and have achieved some major accomplishments since then.

It hasn't always been all roses! I live the life of a gypsy. A 30-day meet here, a 59-day meet there, you're always moving, even before you get a chance to get settled. I bought a home and spend about two months a year living there! I'm so wrapped up in my career that I haven't much time for a social life. No matter what you've done the previous meets, the only thing that matters is "winning" to owners and trainers. If you don't win races, they don't use you, period. So, I'm constantly having to prove myself over and over again. A lot of trainers and owners feel that women are not strong enough to ride horses and "can't finish on a horse!" It's so disappointing to have ridden a good race on a horse only to be taken off and replaced by another (usually male) rider.

I've had several incidences with several jockeys at different times, either during the race or afterwards. At some tracks I ride, there's a lot of professional jealousy. There's always a lot of bumping going on in every race whether intentional or unintentional. I have to let them know I'm not going to be pushed around. Through the years, I've gained the respect of the "respectable" riders, and many others besides. It's always such a fierce competitive atmosphere that sometimes the pressure gets to be too much. A great source of support for me has been my mother who has lived with me for the past seven years. She's "ridden" with me through all the bad and good times of my career, and picks me up when I'm down and gives me that extra push when I need it.

I'm hoping someday I can settle down, have a couple of children and perhaps live a normal life. But then again, there is no bigger thrill in the world than being in the starting gate with 12 other horses and jockeys, sitting astride 1,100 pounds of horse, his heart pounding, nervously dancing in place, waiting (what seems to be an eternity) for that split second when the bell will ring and the doors fly open and you and your horse as one, lunge toward the most exciting one minute, 12 seconds ever imaginable! When you win, you're a hero, when you lose you're a bum. But when you know in your heart that it was you who made the difference in winning a race, it's the most satisfying feeling ever. And no one can ever take that away. As long as I keep winning races everyday, I'm very content with all that goes with living a rewarding and successful life. And I'll keep pursuing my dream to one day be the winner of the Kentucky Derby!

Nita Winter

PHYSICIAN & ASSOCIATE DEAN

Alexandra Mary Levine, 41, is an Executive Associate Dean and Professor of Medicine at the University of Southern California School of Medicine as well as an oncologist.

I am the luckiest person in the world. I love what I do, and come home in the evenings feeling good about myself, feeling as if I really might have made a difference by being alive. My philosophy regarding patient care relates, ultimately, to my philosophy of life. I view life as a series of experiences, leading hopefully, to a depth of perception and understanding relating to the human condition.

As a 16-year-old volunteer at the Los Angeles County/USC Medical Center, I came to realize that a person who is ill or dying is likely to be quite at ease in talking about his or her life experience in detail. If another individual is willing to devote the time to sit and listen, he may become enriched by the experience. I chose to come to USC, and to stay here, because it afforded me the opportunity to understand realities other than my own. I have developed a real appreciation for what life is like, for example, for a recently emigrated Hispanic family, or for a poor Black family from the ghettos of our city, or for the literally hundreds of individuals with whom I have devoted the time in order to become personally enriched.

I view my job as a physician as a give-and-take relationship. I have definitely gained, on a personal basis, from my exposure to the patient, and I thus feel a tremendous sense of responsibility to give back to the best of my abilities. The basis for the finest of doctor/patient relationships involves an appreciation for human-to-human interaction. Health care delivery must start at that point. Acknowledging that I have been enriched by the patient, my responsibility involves further human interaction to provide a sense of peace and comfort. There is a relationship between mind and body. I have seen it over and over, year after year, and have come to accept the relationship, although I cannot explain in scientific terms the mechanism of its action. The art of medicine, it seems to me, involves the understanding and appreciation and use of that relationship to bring a sense of comfort and peace of mind, so that the patient, given the appropriate medication and a little bit of time, may become well again.

Medicine, then, is a thoroughly human profession. As such, it is a natural for a woman. I have never considered myself as a woman doctor, and I secretly resent those who might think of me in those terms. I am a physician, and extraordinarily thankful to be one. I am a woman, and again, most fortunate in that regard as well. I have experienced very little difficulty in my profession because of my sex. But on one such occasion, for example, on my first day of medical school, my assigned laboratory partner told me that he did not at all approve of women in medicine. Although I had no adequate response for some time, I was eventually able to come back to him and explain that if he was threatened by a woman who could do the same as he, then that was his problem, and certainly not mine. Much of what we do and accomplish in life depends upon our attitudes, and our own self-perceptions. If you respect yourself, somehow that respect may be reflected by others. Believe in yourself, and set out to accomplish your goals. Why waste time by believing in failure? Life is too short, and much too sweet and much too precious. If I have learned anything as a physician, I most certainly have learned how fortunate I am, and how important it is to cherish the time which has been given.

Walt Mancini

PASTOR

Kay Francis Albury-Smith, 36, is pastor of Ames United Memorial Methodist Church in Baltimore, Maryland.

Perhaps the greatest tension I experience is the juggling of my time as wife, mother and pastor. Often it seems as though I do none of these tasks well, simply because of the "guilt" that emerges when there doesn't seem to be enough time. Yet in spite of this difficulty, the joys come when my spouse, children and parishoners often tell me how proud and appreciative they are of me. It's worth the struggle.

I had no idea I was going to be a minister, but I've been curious about God/human relationships for a long time, ever since I was a child. My grandmother was a fundamentalist in terms of her understanding of judgment and that's really had an impression on me. But when I preach, I don't tell people they need to know the Lord because of judgment day; I come from the opposite way and say it is because of God's love for us. I first felt the need to preach at the age of 23. I was working with the Washington D.C. Manpower in a good paying job, when I asked myself the ultimate question if there was more to life than my job. At the same time, I was involved with the life of the Methodist Church and I saw a group of young women who were former drug addicts, do a song and witness, and that was almost like a turning point for me. I figured I didn't have those problems, and if God could do that for them, who knows what God could do for me. It's been a spiritual journey of searching and wanting to be active in a church. I wanted to understand a lot of what we say in ritual and personally live that out.

My denomination ordains and appoints women. But it's one thing to be appointed, and another to be accepted. I've learned to not focus on the point that I am a woman, but that I am their pastor. I don't bring that as an issue, and if it's an issue, it's theirs, not mine. I have an assistant pastor who is a woman and she has been with the parish for a long time. One of the difficulties that is quite subtle among my colleagues is the question of whether I'm "tough" enough for such a job, especially a church with more than 600 members. One person had allegedly said that, "Ames was a man's church." Well, it's been a year now and I haven't discovered anything yet that's too hard to pray over, love, nurture, and grow with. It's been a great experience, and I'm looking forward to greater heights.

As a pastor, the biggest challenge I see is offering people alternatives. Today people choose drugs and violence to deal with life issues, especially in the Black community. I feel we have to address the issues that hurt and we often don't address those hard issues. There's some movement in the Black community to build a coalition, but I also feel overwhelmed by the crisis of the Black family and the community. We need to get the people in the church to realize how much we are a part of each other, even though we may not live in the community, it's still our problem and people are still an extension of ourselves.

I'm busy and have long hours and that is a serious problem with family and marriage. I really have to work on that because I have a lot of control over my time. One thing that has happened in the past year is that we lost our 14-year-old son who died of cancer. I have worked out my grief by long hours and over scheduling myself. I'm coming to grips with that now. A lot of what I do is really left up to me. There are some meetings I have to be at, but I can have fewer working hours and be more flexible.

In the final analysis, I believe that women bring a special "touch" to ministry, and we definitely need more Black women in ministry. As women, we're given permission to say, "I don't know," or "I hurt," or "I'm afraid," which often breaks the barriers between clergy and laity. This often allows and nurtures relationships of reconciliation and love, whereby all involved can identify with their human, common struggle with brokenness and the need to be healed. The ministry is a very lonely profession unless we learn how to make friends and learn how to be nurtured and then to nurture others. As ministers, we often feel that we have so much to give to people, but people also have so much to give to us. *All* stand in need of being included, provided for, affirmed, forgiven and free to nurture their gifts all of the time. It's a continuous cycle of redemptive life.

George W. Holsey

WRITER & POET

Meridel LeSueur, 86, has been a writer most of her life, and continues to write daily, living in Minnesota.

When I was ten years old in 1910 I knew my two brothers could be anything they wanted. I knew I could be a wife and mother, a teacher, a nurse or a whore. And without an education, I could not be a nurse or teacher and we were very poor. Women could be china painters, quilt makers, embroiderers. They often wrote secretly. Even read certain books secretly. My mother tried to go to college and women could not take math or history, only the domestic sciences.

I began to write down what I heard, sitting under the quilting frames. I tried to listen to these imprisoned and silenced women. I had a passion to be witness and recorder of the hidden, submerged and silent women. I did not want to be a writer; I did not know a woman writer; I did not read a woman writer. It was a thick, heavy silence and I began to take down what I heard.

My Gramma hated my writing. "We have tried to hide what has happened to us," she said, "and now you are going to tell it." "I am. I am going to tell it," I cried, and I began a long howl and cry that finally found its voice in the women's movement, as it is called. A book I wrote in 1930, cruelly criticized by male editors, was not published until 1975. My audience was women, who now wanted to talk, bear witness.

I made my living working in factories, writing for the labor movement. A good thing for a writer to keep close to life, to the happening, and I have lived in the most brutal century of two world wars, millions killed and exploited, and now the atom bomb and the global struggle.

I went last July to the International Women's Conference in Nairobi at 85 years old to see the thousands of women now bearing their own witness and I read my poem *Solidarity,* which I wrote for the Vietnamese Women's Union, and it was translated at once into Swahili as I read it. A great climax to my life. I believe this is the most enlightened moment I have seen in history and rooted in my life's passion to bear witness to the common struggle, the heroic people rising out of the violence, all becoming visible and alive.

My struggle was never alone, always with others. This makes my life bright with comradeship, marches with banners, tribal courage, and warmth. Remember, I didn't vote 'til I was 19 in 1919. Women only came into the offices after the First World War. Every young man I knew in high school never returned. The fathers and husbands had been killed. A terrible reaction set in after that bloody war to consolidate patriarchal money and power. The twenties were a terrible sinking into the Depression.

My mother, wanting to be an actress, sent me to dramatic school. I tried to fulfill her desires. The theater then was developing actresses who exploited the sexist feminine, and males who had to be John Waynes. The plays were also made for this image of sexism. Coming from the prairies, I played Lady Windermeres Fan by Oscar Wilde, learning to walk and use a fan and speak Britain. I didn't cotton to that at all. I went to Hollywood where again, your career was based on sexism, the female stereotypes. You had to go every morning to the hiring hall and show your legs and teeth and get a job for the day signing a contract that if you were killed or injured the company would not be responsible. Many extras were killed. You were a dime a dozen and the studios were flooded with the beautiful prairie girls from the Midwest. It was a meat market and developed one of the greatest prostitute rings between Los Angeles, San Francisco, Seattle and Las Vegas.

My first job was to jump off a burning ship into salt water with dangerous tides. I lived. You could make $25 a day, an enormous sum, and I could save it and hole in and write for a few months. So I began to write about the open market on women; cheap labor of women, oppression and silencing and bartering of women. Also, fighting in the unions and housing. In the Depression, women were not on any list. There were no soup kitchens for women. Also, there was the danger of sterilization. Groups of women were netted and taken to women's prisons and might be sterilized by morning. There was a theory that the only solution to depression was sterilization of the workers. It began to be known Hitler had the same idea.

In desperation, I think, I boldly had two children at the beginning of the Depression. You couldn't get any other kind of life, and you might give birth to friends and allies. I had two girls, who all my life, have been just that.

I became a correspondent from the Middle West, reporting on the farmers' struggles, the third party, all that was happening. I wrote for several national magazines and began to have stories in American Mercury, and university quarterlies, and writing about my children sold to the women's magazines. So I began to make a modest living at writing, which was wonderful.

I became known as a witness, as I wanted to be. I became well known for two pieces: *Corn Village,* about the small town; and, *I Was Marching,* about the '34 teamsters' strike.

I feel we must be deeply rooted in the tribal family and in the social community. This is becoming a strong and beautiful force now in our societies. Women speaking out boldly, going to jail for peace and sanctuary, defending the children against hunger. We still get half of what men get. But as I saw in Nairobi, the struggle of women is now global. My Gramma and mother are not anymore silenced and alone. Writing has become with women not a concealment, but an illumination. We are not alone. The hundreds of women writers now who speak for us to a large audience.

Margaret Randall

This makes me write more than I ever did. I have 140 notebooks, my letter to the world, published some day for a new woman I dreamed of. I have 24 great grandchildren who have freedoms I could only dream of. One granddaughter is raising five children herself. Another has two sons. They are not alone; that's the point. They live in collectives and work in social fields with women and children. They have an independence I never had, a boldness and a communal life and support.

I am writing as I never wrote before. I have three books, besides my notebooks, to "finish." I call it getting in my crop before the frost! It is my best writing, I believe . . . I have learned to bear witness with love and compassion and warm readers to whom I am truthful. And they return my witness, so women rise from the darkness singing together, not the small and tortured chorus of my grandmothers, but millions becoming visible and singing.